# Using Idi

*A Learner's Gu*

GW01047066

**Other titles of interest include**

HEATON, J. B.
*Exercises in Using Idioms*

LEE, W. R.
*Study Dictionary of Social English*

# Using Idioms
## *A Learner's Guide*

J.B. Heaton

and

T.W. Noble

ENGLISH LANGUAGE TEACHING

**Prentice Hall**
New York  London  Toronto  Sydney  Tokyo

First published 1987 by
Prentice Hall International (UK) Ltd,
66 Wood Lane End, Hemel Hempstead,
Hertfordshire, HP2 4RG
A division of
Simon & Schuster International Group

Printed and bound in Great Britain by
A. Wheaton & Co. Ltd, Exeter.

---

**Library of Congress Cataloging-in-Publication Data**

Heaton, John Brian.
Using idioms
Includes index
1. English language–Idioms.   2. English language–
Conversation and phrase books.   I. Noble, T.W.
II. Heaton, John Brian.   III. Title.
PE1460.H434   1986   428.3'4   86-8176

ISBN 0-13-939505-9

---

**British Library Cataloguing in Publication Data**

Heaton, J.B.
Using idioms: a learner's guide
1. English language—Idioms—Dictionaries
I. Title   II. Noble, T.W.
423'.1   PE1460

ISBN 0-13-939505-9

---

2 3 4 5   92 91 90 89 88

# CONTENTS

# ACKNOWLEDGMENTS

# ACKNOWLEDGEMENTS

The authors wish to acknowledge the valuable help of Dr Helen Potts in assisting with the arrangement of the entries in the initial stages and also the very considerable work of Ms Christine Dean in compiling the Index of Idioms and in typing all the versions of the manuscript at the various stages in the production of this book. Finally, grateful appreciation must be expressed to Mr Donald Adamson for his extremely useful and painstaking help in the editing and checking of the entries. His work has greatly improved the Guide, but the authors take full responsibility for any errors remaining.

# HOW TO USE THIS BOOK

The unique feature of this book is the classification of idioms along functional/notional lines. This allows you to see, at a glance, idioms which have similar meanings or which are related in some way. Such an arrangement provides a new way of presenting idioms, giving ready access to the most appropriate idioms required in particular contexts. In this way, the book encourages a more active and productive approach than that found in existing, more traditional dictionaries of idioms.

Not all idioms fit neatly into one functional/notional category or another. For example, the idiom *on the ball* could be included under *Ability* or *Cleverness* or *Knowledge, Awareness*. An index of the idioms, in alphabetical order, is therefore also included.

**Index of Functions/Notions**
This will help you locate related idioms to express desired functions or notions. For example, you could locate idioms connected with *agreeing, anger, difficulty, excitement,* and so on.

**Entries by Function/Notion**
This section is the main body of the book, to which each index will refer you. Each idiom is followed by a definition and an example of its use in context. Sometimes a ⚠ symbol is given to indicate where particular care should be taken in use, since the idiom might be offensive in some circumstances.

It should be stressed that idioms vary in their suitability for different situations; to grade them according to style and register would, therefore, be subjective. Whereas we should not wish to discourage you from experimenting with the idioms, it is important to realise that correct and appropriate use of them usually only comes with confidence in, and familiarity with, the language.

**Index of Idioms**
This is to help you find and understand a particular idiom you have seen or heard. You should look for the key noun (or the first key

noun) contained in the idiom. If an idiom contains no key nouns, then look for the key verb, adjective, adverb or preposition in the idiom — strictly in this order.

For example: put someone behind **bars** (**bars** = key noun)
            **hit** it off with someone (**hit** = key verb)
            make oneself **scarce** (**scarce** = key adjective)
            do **well** by someone (**well** = key adverb)
            hard **up** (**up** = key preposition)

This index also shows basic stress patterns, the stressed part being underlined.

J.B.H.
T.W.N.

# INDEX OF FUNCTIONS/NOTIONS

Numbers refer to sections, *not* pages

1

# ENTRIES BY FUNCTION/NOTION

## 1. ABILITY

1.1 **on the ball**
        able to do one's job well, very efficient, alert
        *The new clerk is really **on the ball**. He's already improved the filing sytem in the office.*

1.2 **be/get on top of** something
        be able to control or deal with something difficult, etc.
        *This is a difficult job but I'm sure that Mr Lee is **on top of** it from the excellent reports I've had.*

1.3 **get/have the hang of** something/doing something
        develop/have the ability to do or understand something
        *You'll find this car difficult to drive at first. But don't worry: you'll soon **get the hang of** it.*

1.4 **turn** one's **hand to** something
        (begin to) do something for which one is not trained
        *I'll ask Bill to repair the washing machine. He can **turn his hand to** almost any job in the house.*

1.5 **get** one's **eye in**
        become skilful or develop the ability to do something after a period of play or practice
        *John isn't playing very well at the moment, but I'm sure he'll soon **get his eye in** and play as well as he usually does.*

1.6 **get into** one's **stride**
        **get into the swing** of things/something
        reach the stage where one does something very ably or well, become accustomed to doing something so that one does it well
        *It may take Helen a long time to do the job now, but soon she'll work much faster when she has **got into her stride/the swing** of it.*

1.7 **find** one's **feet**
        reach the stage where one is able to do something on one's own
        *I was very grateful to Mr Robinson during my first week in my new job: he helped me a lot until I **found my feet**.*

1.8 **spread/stretch** one's **wings**
        put to use or try out one's own abilities
        *You can't do everything for your children: there comes a time when they must leave home and **spread their wings**.*

1.9 **come into** one's **own**
        come into a situation where one can use one's abilities, talents, etc.; be recognised for them
        *Once the topic of conversation turned to sport, Alan **came into his own** and started talking in a very interesting way.*

3

1.10  **give a good/excellent account of** oneself
Opposite: **give a poor/disappointing account of** oneself
do something well, especially in a competition, etc.
*Rosemary **gave a good account of herself** in the tennis finals and almost won.*

1.11  **have it in one**
have a natural ability (to do something)
*Mr Lee doesn't **have it in him** to be a successful businessman.*

1.12  **keep** one's **hand in**
keep up one's ability to do something by continuing to practise it
*I generally spend a few hours each week painting: I like to **keep my hand in**.*

1.13  **put** someone/something **through** his/her/its **paces**
make someone/something show what he/she/it can do (as a test of ability)
*You can judge for yourself how clever my horse is. Just watch as I **put it through its paces**.*

1.14  **do** one's **stuff**
do something which one is expert at or which one can do well
*You're a good actor, so **do your stuff** and show everybody how well you can perform.*

1.15  **would not put it**/doing something **past** someone
consider someone is capable of doing something (often bad or unusual)
*"Surely Dave didn't tear the page out of this book." "I don't know. I **wouldn't put it past** him.*

1.16  **a past-master**
an expert at something
*Don't believe him: he's **a past-master** at making excuses!*

1.17  **a man Friday/a girl Friday**
a loyal and hardworking assistant who can do different kinds of jobs
*George is **a real man Friday** in my shop. He does all kinds of jobs to help me.*

1.18  **You can't teach an old dog new tricks.**
It is very difficult for old people to develop new abilities, etc.
*He is old, and so you can't expect him to change his ways of doing things. **You can't teach an old dog new tricks**.*


## 2. INABILITY

2.1  **be/get out of** one's **depth**
be in a situation which is too difficult for one to deal with or understand
*Alan has taken a new job with a computer company but is quite **out of his depth** with that kind of work.*

2.2  **be/go/pass (right) above/over** one's **head**
be beyond one's ability to understand
*I'm afraid that most of what Mr Green said about space-shuttle technology **went over my head**.*

2.3  **cannot/will not do** something **to save** one's **life**
be completely unable to do something
*He couldn't repair a watch **to save his life**.*

2.4  **for the life of** one
>    used to emphasise (or show frustration at) one's inability to do
>    something (used in negative statements)
>
>    *For the life of me, I just couldn't move the heavy sofa, no matter how hard I tried.*

2.5  **cannot** do something **for toffee**
>    be unable to do something however hard one tries
>
>    *You surely don't think George could sing in public, do you? He can't sing for toffee!*

2.6  **past it**
>    no longer able to do something (usually because one is too old, too
>    unfit, etc.)
>
>    *Poor chap, he's no longer able to play tennis — he's past it.*

2.7  **a lame duck**
>    someone or something (e.g. a business) unable to survive without help
>
>    *The government refused to invest any more money in a company which never
>    made a profit and which it regarded as a lame duck.*

2.8  **lose the hang of** something/doing something
>    **lose** one's **touch**
>    lose one's skill or ability to do something
>
>    *I haven't enlarged any photographs for a long time. I hope I haven't lost the hang
>    of it.*

2.9  **all fingers and thumbs**
>    unable to do anything practical, i.e. by using one's hands; very
>    clumsy
>
>    *You're all fingers and thumbs: let me tighten the screws for you.*


## 3. CLEVERNESS

3.1  **there are no flies on** someone
>    someone is clever (or cunning) and cannot be deceived (sometimes
>    used in a derogatory way)
>
>    *You'd better tell your neighbour all the facts. Don't try to fool him in any way:
>    there are no flies on him.*

3.2  **have a head for** something
>    have a natural ability to deal with something
>
>    *I don't like climbing mountains — I don't have a head for heights.*

3.3  **have a (good) head on** one's **shoulders**
>    be very clever or shrewd, often in business
>
>    *He must have a good head on his shoulders because he's already started to solve
>    several of the company's problems.*

3.4  **know all the answers/angles**
>    be clever, knowledgeable, shrewd (sometimes used in a derogatory
>    way)
>
>    *John seems to know all the answers, but I don't think he's as clever as he appears
>    at first.*

3.5  **not/never/rarely/seldom miss a trick**
>    be alert and ready to take every opportunity
>
>    *He's a clever salesman. He never misses a trick when dealing with customers.*

3.6   **a whizz kid**
       a bright (young) person (who is soon highly successful in his/her job)
       *He's **a** real **whizz kid**. He's had a lot of brilliant new ideas, and most of them have been successful.*

3.7   **have/keep** one's **wits about** one
       be alert, shrewd and not easily fooled
       *He's the kind of person who will try to cheat you, so **keep your wits about you** when you are dealing with him.*

3.8   **know a thing or two**
       have good judgement, be shrewd
       *She runs a large electronics factory, so she **knows a thing or two** about modern technology.*

## 4. DULLNESS, STUPIDITY

4.1   **slow on the uptake**
       Opposite: **quick on the uptake**
       not alert, slow to learn something
       *I don't think John is very intelligent — he's a bit **slow on the uptake**.*

4.2   **cannot see beyond/further than the end of** one's **nose**
       be incapable of predicting obvious consequences (especially those of one's own actions)
       *He doesn't realise how much damage his reorganisation of the company will cause. He **can't see beyond the end of his nose**.*

4.3   **as thick as two short planks** $\boxed{!}$
       stupid
       *You just can't teach him anything – he's **as thick as two short planks**.*

4.4   **not be all there**
       be slow to understand and lacking in intelligence, judgement, etc.
       *Poor old Bob **isn't** quite **all there**. You must try to explain everything to him extremely slowly and carefully or he won't understand it.*

## 5. EFFORT

5.1   **put** one's **back into** something
       try to work very hard at a job
       *If he is going to make a success of his new job, he really will have to **put his back into** it.*

5.2   **put** one's **heart and soul into** something
       work very hard at something, with a complete belief in the value of what one is doing
       *Charles loved football so much that he always **put his heart and soul into** every game he played.*

5.3   **set/put** one's **mind to** something
       make a very firm decision to do something, concentrate on doing something
       *You will never persuade him to change his plans. Once he has **put his mind to** something, nothing will stop him.*

**5.4** **put** one's **best foot forward**
    try to do something or work as well as one can
    *Put your best foot forward and you'll succeed sooner or later.*

**5.5** **get stuck in**
    start working hard
    *If we all **get stuck in**, we can finish this job today.*

**5.6** **get** one's **teeth into** something
    get beyond the opening stages of a job and work at it in a determined way
    *He'll soon finish now that he's really **got his teeth into** the job.*

**5.7** **keep** one's/someone's **nose to the grindstone**
    keep working hard or make someone work hard
    *Henry's employers **keep his nose to the grindstone** all the time and try to get as much work out of him as possible.*

**5.8** **sweat blood**
    **work** one's **fingers to the bone**
    work very hard
    *In the last century, there were no trade unions, and so workers could be made to **sweat blood**/ to **work their fingers to the bone**.*

**5.9** **break** one's **back**
    work very hard (often used in the negative)
    *Don't **break your back** to finish the work tonight. Tomorrow will be all right.*

**5.10** **be at pains** to do something/**take pains** to do something
    make an effort to do something
    *John was so fond of his teacher that he always **took pains** to please her in every way he could.*

**5.11** **go out of** one's **way** to do something
    make a special effort to do something (usually used to praise someone)
    *He was always prepared to **go out of his way** to please any one he respected.*

**5.12** **do/try** one's **(level) best**
    do everything one can (usually without success)
    *In spite of **doing his level best**, he failed to pass the test.*

**5.13** **on** one's **toes**
    constantly ready for danger, prepared to act quickly
    *We'll have to be **on our toes**: the boss is going to spend the whole day looking round our department.*

**5.14** **make the best of** something
    do the best one can (in a difficult situation)
    *You'll have to go to the party even though you don't want to, so **make the best of it** and enjoy yourself.*

**5.15** **pull out all the stops**
    try as hard as one can to achieve something
    *If our company wants to win this contract, it'll have to **pull out all the stops**. There's a lot of competition for the contract.*

**5.16** **by hook or by crook**
    with every possible effort, by any means at all (rather dated)
    *I'll solve this problem **by hook or by crook** — even if I have to stay up all night or ask all my friends for their help.*

**5.17  leave no stone unturned**
   **leave no avenue unexplored**
   try every possible method of achieving something
   *When investigating the crime, the police **left no stone unturned/left no avenue unexplored** in their efforts to find the criminal.*

**5.18  go through/over something with a fine toothcomb**
   examine something very thoroughly, look at every detail
   *The interviewer **went through** my application form **with a fine toothcomb** before he decided to offer me a job.*

**5.19  move heaven and earth to do something**
   do everything possible to achieve something (usually by talking to people, etc.)
   *Mr Morris said he was going to **move heaven and earth** to persuade the committee to buy the new machine.*

**5.20  full speed/steam ahead**
   as fast or as hard as possible
   *It will have to be **full speed/steam ahead** if we are to complete the contract on time.*

**5.21  not do something by halves**
   try to do something thoroughly or well
   *You can rely on Mary: she'll do the job well. She **never does** anything **by halves**.*

**5.22  pull one's socks up**
   make an effort to do better (often used as a warning to a child)
   *He is not doing very well in his new class — he will have to **pull his socks up** if he wants to pass the test.*

**5.23  get/pull one's finger out** ⚠
   stop wasting time and start working
   *Mr Lee told Alan to **pull his finger out** and work hard for a change.*

**5.24  try one's hand at something**
   try to do something (for the first time) to see if one likes it or can do it
   *I am prepared to **try my hand at** writing a speech even though I have never done it before.*

**5.25  have a crack at something**
   make an attempt to do something difficult
   *I will **have a crack at** putting that new part in the car engine — though it is really a job for the garage.*

**5.26  have a go**
   try, make an effort
   *Come on. **Have a go**! You'll soon learn to do it if you try.*

**5.27  spadework**
   hard work done in preparation for something
   *Now that our sales staff have done the **spadework**, we should be able to sell a lot of our goods next year.*

**5.28  donkey work**
   hard, tiring work (usually involving physical labour)
   *I enjoy gardening, but I do like to have someone to do the **donkey work** — digging the soil and weeding.*

**5.29  work like a horse/dog/slave/Trojan**
   work hard

*The men who first built the railways had to **work like Trojans** because they did not have any mechanical tools — only picks and shovels.*

5.30 **not lift a finger/hand** to help/to do something

not make any effort at all to help/to do something

*When my mother comes to stay with us, she expects everything to be done for her — she **won't lift a finger** to help in the house.*

5.31 **bone idle** $\boxed{!}$

very lazy

*You never offer to help your mother. You're **bone idle**!*

# 6. ENERGY

6.1 **a ball of fire**

a person with great energy

*The trainer will have to be **a ball of fire** to get this football team to play well.*

6.2 **full of beans**

very lively and energetic

*Ann is always **full of beans**. She makes every party she gives go well.*

6.3 **burn the candle at both ends**

be continuously active, even at times when one should be resting (i.e. at night)

*He works hard all day and goes to parties every night. He's **burning the candle at both ends**.*

6.4 **still going strong**

still energetic and healthy, efficient and in good working order

*He's eighty-five and **still going strong**.*

*There's no need to replace this lawn-mower: it's **still going strong** even though it's quite old.*

6.5 **going great guns**

proceeding with all one's energy (and with great success)

*This new theatrical company is **going great guns** because the members are so enthusiastic.*

6.6 **get** one's **second wind**

recover one's energy (after having used it up temporarily)

*The runner **got his second wind** after a few miles and was then able to complete the course.*

6.7 **run out of steam**

use up or lose one's energy, become exhausted

*Charlie worked very hard for two hours but he then seemed to **run out of steam**.*

6.8 **elbow grease**

hard work, energy (usually for a job done by hand)

*Use a bit of **elbow grease** the next time you polish the car. Then it'll begin to shine.*

# 7. DIFFICULTY

7.1 **have (all)** one's **work cut out** (for one)

be faced with a very difficult task

*James will **have all his work cut out** to do what you're asking — it's a huge task.*

**7.2  take some/a lot of doing**
be difficult to do
*I'm going to reorganise the company completely, but I know it'll **take some doing**.*

**7.3  find something heavy/hard going**
find that something is difficult or requires a lot of hard work
*If he tries to do it that way, he'll **find it hard going**; there are much easier methods.*

**7.4  bite off more than one can chew**
try to do something more difficult than one is able to do
*Henry is very capable, but I think that this time he has **bitten off more than he can chew**: he has never done this kind of work before.*

**7.5  make heavy weather of something**
have difficulty doing something (and use more effort on it than is really necessary)
*This grammar book goes into far too much detail and **makes heavy weather of** things that could be explained much more simply.*

**7.6  have one's back to/against the wall**
be in a difficult or dangerous situation from which one cannot escape
*Since William took up his new post, he has been attacked on all sides. He really **has his back to the wall**.*

**7.7  have one's hands full**
be very busy
*He **has his hands full** in his new job because his supervisor wants everything done at once.*

**7.8  take the bull by the horns**
deal with a difficult situation in a bold and direct manner
*We decided to **take the bull by the horns** and tell him that he wasn't doing his job properly.*

**7.9  go through the mill**
**put someone through the mill**
experience/make someone experience hardships and difficulties (usually as a test or part of one's training)
*When you join the Army, you have to **go through the mill**, as the training is very severe.*

**7.10  learn/find out/discover something the hard way**
learn from one's own experience or mistakes
*We got very cold and wet the first time we went camping. We **learned the hard way** how important it is to take extra warm clothing.*

**7.11  throw someone in at the deep end**
put someone in a difficult situation without preparing them for it
*When he was appointed the firm's representative in London, he **was thrown in at the deep end**, because he had never done any work like that before.*

**7.12  grin and bear it**
put up with something difficult or unpleasant
*You'll just have to **grin and bear it** until we can repair the light for your room.*

**7.13  easier said than done**
more difficult to do than it may sound
*She told me I could have something to eat if I wanted, but this was **easier said than done** — there was no food in the house.*

**7.14  a tall order**
>  something which one is told to do but which is very difficult
>
>  *It is **a tall order** to expect me to finish the job in two days. It will take a week at least.*

**7.15  the chief/main stumbling block**
>  something which makes it difficult for one to do what one wants
>
>  ***The main stumbling block** in the way of the secretary's proposals is the opposition of the managing director.*

**7.16  teething troubles**
>  difficulties arising at the beginning of an activity
>
>  *Motor manufacturers often have **teething troubles** with some new models because they have not been fully tested.*

**7.17  the (only) fly in the ointment**
>  something unpleasant causing trouble or difficulty in a situation which is otherwise satisfactory
>
>  *I enjoyed the picnic very much. **The only fly in the ointment** was the rude bus-driver who shouted at us.*

**7.18  a fine/pretty kettle of fish**
>  a difficult or awkward situation
>
>  *Having missed the last train of the day, she turned to me and said, "This is **a fine kettle of fish**. Now we can't get home tonight."*

**7.19  a/the devil of a job**
**the devil's own job**
>  a very difficult task
>
>  *I had **the devil of a job** putting this old car in good order.*

**7.20  a hard/tough nut (to crack)**
>  a difficult problem or person to deal with
>
>  *It took a long time for the trade union and the manager of the company to reach agreement. They found the problem a very **tough nut to crack**.*

**7.21  hard put to it**
>  unable to do something, able to do something only with great difficulty
>
>  *I'll be **hard put to it** to find the money to pay for the new car.*

**7.22  in/into a pickle/fix/hole**
>  in a very difficult situation
>
>  *I got myself **into a pickle/fix/hole** by not filling in my work permit correctly.*

**7.23  up the creek/up a gum tree**
>  in trouble, in a difficult situation (sometimes used in a mildly derogatory way)
>
>  *I'm **up a gum tree**. I've no money, and I have to pay the rent by next Friday.*

**7.24  in a tight squeeze**
>  in a difficult situation, usually because of a lack of money
>
>  *John is **in a tight squeeze** and can't really afford to go on holiday.*

**7.25  in a spot of trouble/bother**
>  in trouble, in a difficult or embarrassing position
>
>  *I'm **in a spot of trouble**. I borrowed some equipment from the office, and the manager thinks I stole it.*

**7.26  (skate) on thin ice**
>  (be) in a dangerous situation
>
>  *He has ignored all the warnings I gave him. He's **skating on thin ice**.*

7.27 **in/into deep water(s)**

in difficulties, open to controversy

*David got **into deep water** when he tried to write a newspaper article about the political situation in his country.*

7.28 **hit a snag**

run into a difficulty, be faced with a problem

*The new bus service has **hit a snag** because several buses now need to be repaired at the same time.*


# 8. EASE

8.1 **a piece of cake/child's play**

something very easy to do

*Replacing the plugs in a car engine was **a piece of cake** to an experienced mechanic like Mike.*

*To learn a speech by heart is **child's play** to an experienced actor.*

8.2 **plain sailing**

very easy, causing no problems at all

*It was **plain sailing** to find our way to your village because the signposts were so easy to follow.*

8.3 **(there is) nothing to it**

(it is) very easy

*I'll teach Jenny how to ride a bicycle. **There's nothing to it**.*

8.4 **(take) a short cut**

(use) an easier or faster way to do something

*I want you to do a proper job of repairing my car. Don't **take** any **short cuts**.*

8.5 **clear the way for** something

make it easy for, remove obstacles for

*The government's agreement **cleared the way for** the signing of a peace treaty between the two countries.*

8.6 **(take) the line of least resistance**

(take) the easiest way of doing something

*When asked to do a lot of extra work, he **took the line of least resistance** and agreed, though he would have preferred not to do so.*

8.7 **a/the soft option**

an alternative which is easier or more pleasant to take

*When offered the choice of two plays, the actress took **the soft option** and chose the one she had played in before.*

8.8 **a soft job**

an easy task, job, etc.

*Tina's got a **soft job**: she doesn't start until ten and she finishes at four.*

8.9 **a sitting duck**

an easy target (to shoot at or criticise)

*If he makes stupid statements like that during the debate, he'll be **a sitting duck** for the opposing side.*

8.10 **a soft/easy touch**

someone from whom one can easily get money, etc.

*He has a lot of money and he hates to say "no". Consequently, he is **a soft touch** for anyone wanting a loan.*

8.11 able to do something **with one hand/arm (tied) behind** one's **back**
able to do something without any difficulty
*An experienced car thief could steal this car **with one hand tied behind his back**.*

8.12 able to do something **standing on** one's **head**
able to do something very easily
*Elsie knows so much about packing these goods that she could do it **standing on her head**.*

8.13 **make short work of** something/someone
finish something quickly and easily
*I felt in the mood to finish the task he had given me, and I **made short work of** it.*

8.14 **give/hand** someone/something **on a plate**
let someone have something easily (without having to compete or fight hard for it)
*Our team won 12–1: the other team **handed us** the match **on a plate** — they seemed to accept defeat after the first goal and they never really tried after that.*

8.15 **win hands down**
win without any difficulty, win by a large margin (used about games, etc.)
*Dave **won** the race **hands down** because the other competitors were so poor.*

8.16 **cruise (home) to victory**
win easily, without any great effort (used about games, etc.)
*Having scored four goals in the first half, our team could relax in the second half and still **cruise home to victory**.*

8.17 **Easy come, easy go.**
What was easily earned or obtained can be easily lost or spent
*I sometimes win a lot of money from betting on horses, but I soon spend it. It's a case of **easy come, easy go**.*

8.18 **go/run like clockwork**
go/run smoothly, without difficulty
*The bank robbery **went like clockwork**. The guards didn't discover it until the following morning.*

8.19 **(and) Bob's your uncle!**
used as a comment at the end of a simple, practical task
*So, I tighten the screw this way — and there you are. **Bob's your uncle!***

8.20 **take to** something **like a duck to water**
do something easily and naturally
*He **took to** playing the piano **like a duck to water** — he has a natural gift for music.*

## 9. KNOWLEDGE, AWARENESS

9.1 **know** a place **like the back of** one's **hand**
know a place very well
*Alan is very good at guiding you over these dangerous moors — he **knows** the country **like the back of his hand**.*

9.2 **know what's what**
know how a system works, how things are done
*Once you **know what's what** in the company, you'll be able to take on more responsibility.*

9.3   **know** one's **way (a)round**
      be familiar with a place, a routine, an organisation, a system
      *I like to go to London with Frank because he really does **know his way around**.*

9.4   **know/learn the ropes**
      understand/learn the details or routine of a job, a system, etc.
      *It won't take you long to **learn the ropes** because you've done a similar job before.*

9.5   **know the score**
      know everything about a situation, especially things that ordinary
      people are not aware of
      *The secretary of the meeting **knew the score**. He was well aware that what was
      decided in private was more important that what was said in public.*

9.6   **know the ins and outs**
      know all the details of a system, etc.
      *To keep everything running smoothly, you have to **know the ins and outs** of all the
      processes.*

9.7   **in the know**
      know something which only a small group of people know (and others
      do not know)
      *He has the confidence of the management, and so he is one of the few people who
      are **in the know** about future company policy.*

9.8   **in touch**
      in communication with someone
      *"Have a nice trip. Keep **in touch** while you're away." "I'll write or phone at least
      once a week."*

9.9   **(not) with it**
      (not) alert, fully aware of what is happening (often used in the negative)
      *I'm sorry, but I'm **not** quite **with it** this morning. I was up very late last night.*

9.10  **have** something **at** one's **fingertips**
      know a lot about a subject so that one does not need to spend time
      checking up on one's facts
      *Dr Roberts was able to answer a lot of questions after the lecture because he **had**
      so much knowledge **at his fingertips**.*

9.11  **have/keep** one's **finger on the pulse of** something
      know exactly what is happening in an organisation, etc.
      *The chairman does his best to **keep his finger on the pulse of** his company's
      activities.*

9.12  **keep track of** someone/something **keep tabs on** someone/something
      keep oneself informed about someone or something
      *I can't **keep track of** David: he's always changing jobs.*
      *It would pay you to **keep tabs on** Charlie – he is unpredictable and unreliable.*

9.13  **have/get** someone/something **taped**
      know or understand all about a person or a situation
      *I've got Sam **taped** — I know exactly what he's trying to do.*

9.14  **read** someone **like a book**
      know or understand a person extremely well
      *I know his habits so well that I can **read him like a book**.*

9.15  have a **nodding acquaintance with** someone/something
      know someone/something but not very well
      *We only have a **nodding acquaintance with** Fred as we've met him twice.*

9.16 **a household word/name**
     someone or something very widely known
     *The product has become so famous that its brand name has now become **a household word**.*

9.17 **get the picture/message**
     understand the situation, know what one is supposed to do
     *"Do you want me to explain it further?" "No, it's O.K. I've **got the message**."*

9.18 **the penny drops**
     used when someone suddenly understands something that should have been obvious
     *I hadn't realised that Tom was in love with Mary, but when I saw how he looked at her **the penny** finally **dropped**.*

9.19 **see the light**
     change one's beliefs about something (e.g. a religion, a political movement)
     *John used to be very much against our political party, but now he's **seen the light** and come over to our side.*

9.20 **open** someone's **eyes to** something
     make someone aware (of something usually unpleasant)
     *The evidence I heard against James **opened my eyes to** his true character.*

9.21 **with** one's **eyes wide open**
     fully aware of a situation, without false ideas
     *Mary knows very well how bad-tempered Tom is, and so when she marries him it will be **with her eyes wide open**.*

9.22 **bring** something **home to** someone
     make someone fully realise or understand something
     *That long ride on horseback **brought home to me** the difficulties of travel several hundred years ago.*

9.23 **get** something **straight**
     make sure something is completely understood
     *Now **get this straight** — you must never take my car again without first asking me.*

# 10. IGNORANCE

10.1 **not know a thing/the first thing about** something
     know nothing at all about something
     *How can Mr Wright give a lecture about the French economy? He **doesn't know the first thing about** it.*

10.2 **not know/tell one end of** something **from the other**
     know nothing at all about (a machine, a tool, etc.)
     *Some people **don't know one end of** a car **from the other** and have to get a mechanic to do the simplest work.*

10.3 **not make head or tail of** something/someone
     not understand anything at all about something or someone
     *I read Mr Smith's latest book on advanced technology but **couldn't make head or tail of** many of his theories.*

10.4 **not have a clue**
     not know at all, have no idea
     *When the car broke down, Ted **didn't have a clue** what to do.*

10.5 **not know** someone **from Adam**

not recognise or know someone at all

*I don't know him from Adam — I haven't seen him before.*

10.6 **His/The/etc. left hand doesn't know what his/the/etc. right hand is doing.**

One section of an operation, business, etc. does not know what another section is doing.

*Most government departments have no contact with other departments. The **left hand never knows what the right hand is doing.***

10.7 **it's all Greek to me/him/etc.**

It's too hard for me/him/etc. to understand

*Computer language may be very necessary but **it's all Greek to me** — I cannot understand any of it.*

10.8 **it's anybody's guess**

I don't know

*It's anybody's guess where John's gone. I've simply got no idea at all.*

10.9 **there's no telling**

no one knows

***There's no telling** how many people will attend the meeting.*

10.10 **if** someone **had half an eye**

if a person were willing to notice a situation (i.e. if he/she were not so stupidly unaware)

*If the management **had half an eye**, they would see that there's going to be trouble in the company this year.*

10.11 **talk through** one's **hat**

talk nonsense (without being aware of the facts)

*Don't **talk through your hat**: you don't know anything about the subject.*

10.12 **at** one's **wit's end**

not knowing what to do (when faced with a difficult situation)

*He is **at his wit's end** — he has no money and nowhere to live.*

10.13 **an unknown quantity**

someone or something that little or nothing is known about

*We don't know Mr Jones at all, and so we don't know how he'll vote at the meeting. He's **an unknown quantity**.*

10.14 **keep/leave** someone **in the dark**

keep/leave someone ignorant about something, not knowing what is happening

*Mr Todd is quite prepared to do things his own way and to **leave** everyone else **in the dark** as to what is happening.*

10.15 **(live) in cloud cuckoo land**

be ignorant of reality, live in a totally unrealistic world

*The Prime Minister was accused of **living in cloud cuckoo land** and being completely unaware of the poverty in the country.*

10.16 **bury** one's **head in the sand**

refuse to face up to a difficult situation

*Edward is a fool to **bury his head in the sand**: he ought to face up to his problems and start dealing with them.*

10.17 **the blind leading the blind**

people who know little or nothing about something being guided by others who also know little or nothing about it

*The headmaster told the teachers how to deal with the trouble in the school, but he really had no better idea than they had: it was a case of **the blind leading the blind**.*

## 11. INTUITION

11.1 **feel (it) in** one's **bones**
know something intuitively, suspect something (without any knowledge of the facts)
*I **feel it in my bones** that our team is going to win tomorrow. I don't know why — it's just a feeling I have.*

11.2 **deep down/in** one's **heart of hearts**
in one's deepest feelings and thoughts
*I hope Vincent will pass the examination, but **deep down** I'm fairly sure he'll fail.*

## 12. ATTENTION

12.1 **have/keep** an/one's **ear to the ground**
pay close attention to something that is happening, especially things that have not yet been discussed publicly
*Bill knows a great deal about the work of the Council because he **keeps his ear to the ground** and picks up a lot of information.*

12.2 **keep** an/one's **eye on** someone/something
watch someone/something carefully
*Please **keep your eye on** the new worker we engaged yesterday — he will require some supervision.*

12.3 **hang on** someone's **words/hang on every word**
listen attentively and with total belief in what someone says
*The speaker was very persuasive: by the end of the lecture the audience were **hanging on every word** he said.*

12.4 **all ears**
eager to listen to every word someone says
*I heard my name mentioned in a conversation behind me, and so I was **all ears**.*

12.5 **all eyes**
looking at something with close attention
*The small girl was **all eyes** when she saw the dolls.*

12.6 **catch** someone's **eye**
attract someone's attention (by causing him/her to look at one)
*I must **catch the eye** of the girl over there — I particularly want to speak to her.*

12.7 **Look here!**
used to get someone's attention, usually to make a complaint, etc.
***Look here!** This meal is not up to standard and I want my money back.*

12.8 **go in (through/at) one ear and out (of/at) the other**
not receive someone's full attention, make little impression
*Alan never remembers anything you tell him. It **goes in one ear and out the other**.*

12.9 **turn a deaf ear** (to someone/a request)
refuse to pay any attention to a person's words or to a request
*He **turned a deaf ear** to my request for more money and I didn't get any increase in salary.*

12.10  **turn a blind eye**

ignore behaviour which is against the rules or illegal (especially behaviour which one approves of)

*The police **turned a blind eye** to the fact that the thief had been beaten up by the owner of the house.*

12.11  **close/shut** one's **eyes to** something

pretend to have no knowledge of what is happening (especially if one disapproves of it)

*The manager must have suspected that someone in the office was a thief, but he **closed his eyes to** it.*

## 13. DISCOVERY, FINDING OUT

13.1  **get wind of** something

hear about something which was meant to be a secret, etc., hear unofficially

*I visited the company's works last week and **got wind of** a new car they are producing.*

13.2  **see/find out how/which way the wind blows/is blowing**

observe signs of what people are thinking or what will happen (before deciding to do something)

*Before we decide on our election campaign, we shall have to **see which way the wind blows** by interviewing a large number of voters.*

13.3  **see/find out/discover how the land lies**

learn more about a situation (before deciding to do something)

*See the committee and **find out how the land lies** before putting forward your proposal.*

13.4  **get** something **straight from the horse's mouth**

(find out something) from the original source (i.e. the person directly concerned)

*"How did you know about Harold's resignation?" "I **got it straight from the horse's mouth** — he told me himself."*

13.5  **read between the lines**

learn something from what words suggest indirectly rather than what they say directly

*Ann says her business trip went well. But **reading between the lines** of her report, I can see there were a lot of problems*

13.6  **come to light**

be discovered, be made generally known

*The mistake **came to light** when we discovered that there were a thousand extra copies of the book in the bookstore.*

13.7  **pick** someone's **brains**

find out information from someone (by asking questions, etc.)

*If we are to start the new process, we shall have to **pick the brains** of those who have had some experience of doing the job.*

13.8  **catch** someone **in the act/catch** someone **red-handed**

discover someone actually doing something wrong or unlawful

*The guards **caught** the assassin **in the act/caught** the assassin **red-handed**: he was about to fire the gun at the President when they seized him.*

13.9    **catch** someone **with** his **pants/trousers down**
find someone in an unprepared (often embarrassing) position
*The security guards were **caught with their trousers down**. They were smoking and playing cards when the police told them the premises had been broken into.*

# 14. THINKING, CONSIDERING

14.1    **jump to conclusions/the wrong conclusion/the conclusion that. . .**
reach a decision without considering something carefully (or having any proof)
*The next time you see my car, don't **jump to the conclusion that** I am the driver. My daughter often drives it.*

14.2    **beat** one's **brains/rack** one's **brains**
think a lot or worry a lot about something
*I spent the whole night **racking my brains**, trying to find a solution to the problem.*

14.3    **cross** one's **mind**
occur to one, come into someone's thoughts
*It **crossed my mind** that he was dealing with the matter in a very foolish way.*

14.4    **always at the back of** one's **mind**
never completely absent from one's thoughts
*I didn't actually ask him for money, but the idea was **always at the back of my mind** when I was talking to him.*

14.5    **a bee in** one's **bonnet**
an idea or subject one is always thinking or talking about (usually used in a derogatory way)
*Mrs Brown has **a bee in her bonnet** about people drinking a lot of coffee – she thinks it is most unhealthy.*

14.6    **(speak) off the cuff**
**(speak/talk) off the top of** one's **head**
(speak/talk) without thinking carefully first, without any preparation
*I haven't read her report in detail, but speaking **off the top of my head**, I'd say that most of her ideas are very good.*

14.7    **use** one's **loaf**
think carefully, be sensible
*Open the window this way! See how easy it is if you **use your loaf**!*

14.8    **think better of** something
decide not to do something (usually after careful consideration)
*On further consideration, I **thought better of** my original decision to vote against the proposal.*

14.9    **think twice**
consider something again, consider something very carefully (and usually reach a different decision, opinion, etc.)
*The next time, **think twice** before telling Mary any secrets: she'll probably tell all her friends.*

14.10    **(on) second thoughts**
after considering something once again
*All right, I'll come with you now. No, **on second thoughts**, I'll stay a little longer and come home by taxi.*

14.11 **in the light of** something
       after considering the evidence of
       *In the light of what the various speakers have had to say, I have changed my decision.*

14.12 **be with it/me/etc.**
       be able to understand something/someone, be able to think clearly about something
       *Do you understand what I've been saying? Are you still with me?*

14.13 **frame of mind**
       way of thinking, temporary attitude, mood
       *I'm in no frame of mind to listen to any more excuses.*

14.14 **A penny for your thoughts.**
       Tell us what you are thinking about.
       *A penny for your thoughts! You're obviously thinking deeply about something and we would like to know what it is.*

## 15. JUDGEMENT

15.1 **get/take** someone's **measure**
     **get/take the measure of** someone
     judge a person's character or abilities, form an opinion of someone
     *Now that I've got the measure of him, I feel more confident about speaking against him in the debate.*

15.2 **in** someone's **book**
     in someone's opinion or judgement
     *In my book, Mr Thornton would be just the right person to run the new hotel: he's got so much experience.*

15.3 **hit the nail on the head**
     say something that is exactly right about something
     *You hit the nail on the head when you said that George was lazy. He has always been like that.*

15.4 **strike the right note**
     say something that has the right effect (usually in a speech or letter)
     *Miss Lee struck exactly the right note when she mentioned Mr Green's problems: she said a few words but didn't cause embarrassment.*

15.5 **have an eye for** something/**have an ear for** something
     have an appreciation of something artistic or musical, be a good judge of it
     *Henry has an eye for antique vases: his collection is beautiful.*
     *Do you have a good ear for music?*

## 16. SENSE

16.1 **have** one's **head screwed on (the right way)**
     be sensible, clever, shrewd
     *Paul has his head screwed on the right way, and I trust his judgement*

16.2 **have/keep** one's **feet (set/planted) (firmly) on the ground**
     be practical, realistic
     *Mrs Low keeps her feet planted firmly on the ground. She never gets carried away by the enthusiasm of those around her.*

16.3 **bring** someone **to his/her senses**
cause someone to abandon a foolish plan or course of action
*Margaret is spending too much money, and it is time she was **brought to her senses**.*

16.4 **keep/have a level head**
keep/be calm or sensible
*He **kept a level head** after the accident and informed both the police and the hospital.*

16.5 **within reason**
in a sensible (not an extreme) way, not going beyond what is expected or what is sensible
*You can claim all your expenses **within reason** but don't travel first class.*

## 17. MADNESS, FOLLY

17.1 **round the bend/twist** ☐!
**off** one's **head/nut/rocker** ☐!
**not right in the head** ☐!
mad, crazy
*Judging by the silly way he behaved at the party, he must be **round the bend/off his nut**/etc.*

17.2 **not in** one's **right mind**
mad, not sensible
*The fact that he has declined such a wonderful offer shows that he is **not in his right mind**.*

17.3 **out of** one's **mind/senses**
mad, crazy, totally confused
*Harry must be **out of his mind** to consider playing football again at the age of 50!*

17.4 **have a screw loose/missing** ☐!
be a little mad, not quite sane
*Anyone who considers crossing the Atlantic in a bath must **have a screw loose**.*

17.5 **He/she/etc. should/ought to/needs to have his/her/etc. head examined/ tested/seen to** ☐!
used to comment on someone who is acting in a mad or stupid manner
*Did you see the way he was driving that car? **He ought to have his head examined**.*

17.6 **a mug's game**
something which only a fool would do
*Betting on horses is **a mug's game**: no one ever wins.*

## 18. POSSIBILITY

18.1 **on the cards**
possible, likely
*It is **on the cards** that he will be invited to join the new government as he is very friendly with the president.*

18.2 **not have a/the ghost of a chance**
not have even a slight possibility (of doing something)
*Mary **doesn't have a ghost of a chance** of winning the competition. I'm afraid the opposition is much too strong.*

18.3    do something **on the off-chance**
        do something because there is a (slight) possibility (that something will
        happen)
        *He took a risk and bought the business **on the off-chance** that it would do well.*

18.4    **a sporting chance**
        reasonable possibility
        *I think you have **a sporting chance**: you'll certainly win if Tom is not on his best
        form.*

18.5    **the odds/chances are**
        the possibility is
        ***The odds/chances are** that our team will finish at the top of the league table, as our
        remaining matches aren't too difficult.*

18.6    **stand to**
        be likely to
        *They **stand to** lose thousands of pounds if the business fails.*


# 19. IMPOSSIBILITY

19.1    **out of the question**
        impossible, not even to be considered
        *Marriage is **out of the question** — I do not love you.*

19.2    **no go**
        impossible, not allowed
        *"Can you come round for lunch on Tuesday?" "**No go**, I'm afraid — I shall be
        working."*

19.3    **Pigs might/could fly (if they had wings).**
        Used about anything considered impossible or highly unlikely to
        happen
        *He talks about crossing the Sahara Desert on foot. Well, **pigs might fly (if they had
        wings)**.*


# 20. CERTAINTY

20.1    **bound to**
        certain to (do something)
        *You're **bound to** get a seat if you arrive early.*

20.2    **no question of**
        no possibility of, no need for discussion about
        *There's **no question of** you not coming: we shan't go without you.*

20.3    **in the bag**
        certain, sure
        *Winning this game is **in the bag** — we're leading by five goals to nil.*

20.4    **you can bet your life**
        **you can bet your bottom dollar**
        you can be absolutely sure
        *You can **bet your life/bet your bottom dollar** that he'll be playing again as soon as
        he recovers from his injury. George won't give up.*

20.5  **as likely/like as not**
almost certainly
*As **likely/like as not**, the price of petrol will soon go up again.*

20.6  **a hot favourite**
someone/something that is very likely to achieve something or be chosen for something
*Jacobson's novel 'Scarlet Spring' is **a hot favourite** to win the National Literature Prize this year.*

20.7  **There are no two ways about it.**
It is certain. It is definite
*The company is slowly going bankrupt, and we'll have to look for another job. **There are no two ways about it.***

20.8  **I'll eat my hat**
I'll be very surprised (if something unlikely happens).
*I'll **eat my hat** if that horse wins the race! It's got no chance at all.*

20.9  **Make no mistake about it.**
It is certain. There is no doubt about it.
*Thomas will cause a lot of trouble if he is made manager. **Make no mistake about it.***

# 21. UNCERTAINTY, DOUBT

21.1  **touch and go**
uncertain, doubtful, risky
*It was **touch and go** as to whether the lifeboat would reach the sinking ship in time to rescue the crew.*

21.2  **in the air**
1 uncertain, undecided
2 fairly likely to happen
*1 Future developments in education are still **in the air**. The new government has not made any decisions about them yet.*
*2 There are some important new production methods **in the air**. These ideas will be put into effect soon.*

21.3  **in the lap of the gods**
completely uncertain, a matter of fate
*No one knows whether or not the king will recover from his illness. It is now **in the lap of the gods**.*

21.4  **hit-or-miss**
uncertain, without proper planning
*The teachers did not have time to plan their courses for the new examination, and so their teaching was a **hit-or-miss** affair.*

21.5  **a leap in the dark**
an action with uncertain results
*The unusual design of the new boat is **a leap in the dark** by the shipbuilders. However, they think it may prove very successful.*

21.6  **take pot luck**
be uncertain about what one will get but be willing to accept it
*Stay and have a meal with us — if you don't mind **taking pot luck**. We've got some food in the fridge but I'm not certain what it is.*

21.7 **take** something **with a pinch of salt**
not believe all of what one is told about something
*Did she tell you that she lost money when she sold her car? If I were you, I'd take that with a pinch of salt — I'm sure she got a good price for it.*

21.8 **at a loss**
uncertain what to say or do
*I've done all I can to repair this engine, but without success. I'm completely at a loss to know what to do.*

21.9 **not know which way to turn**
be uncertain or confused about what to do next
*I've tried to find various solutions to this problem, but none seem to work. I don't know which way to turn.*

21.10 **in two minds**
uncertain whether to do something or not
*I am in two minds about whether to go. I want to but I really think I ought to stay.*

21.11 **at sixes and sevens**
uncertain and confused
*We lost the match because we were all at sixes and sevens. There was no organisation or planning in the way we played.*

## 22. CHANCE, LUCK

22.1 **chance** one's **arm**
take a risk by trying to do something new or difficult
*Mary is chancing her arm by taking on this difficult job because she has no training for it.*

22.2 **take** a/one's **chance/trust to luck**
rely on one's luck, leave to fate
*We'll have to take a chance/trust to luck about getting home after this meeting. There won't be any buses.*

22.3 **stick** one's **neck out**
take a great risk, especially by doing or saying something which may cause trouble or which later may be proved wrong
*He is sticking his neck out by being so frank and critical. I doubt if many people will support him.*

22.4 **put all** one's **eggs in/into one basket**
risk everything on one thing only
*George has put all his eggs into one basket. He's used all his savings to buy this small shop.*

22.5 **hedge** one's **bets**
Opposite: **put all** one's **eggs in/into one basket**
try to avoid losing money, etc. by taking care not to risk everything on only one thing
*Harry Smith is hedging his bets by finding several customers for his goods. If one fails, he can rely on the others.*

22.6 **put** one's **shirt** on something
risk everything one has (especially by betting on something)
*I'd put my shirt on this product because I know it is better than anything else on the market.*

**22.7**    **push** one's **luck**

take too great a risk, often after having already successfully taken a risk

*You have already been given two extra workers to help you. Don't push your luck by asking for more.*

**22.8**    **risk** one's **neck**

take a great risk, especially with one's life or something extremely important

*A racing driver is constantly risking his neck, particularly when the race circuit is wet.*

**22.9**    **neck or nothing**

used to refer to a situation where one risks everything

*It's neck or nothing. I must win tonight if I am to keep my reputation as the best player in the country.*

**22.10**    **a long shot/a shot in the dark**

a guess (usually based on little or no information), an attempt or plan unlikely to succeed

*It's a long shot/a shot in the dark but it's just possible you may be able to obtain spare parts for your car from that garage over there.*

**22.11**    **not have a hope/chance in hell** ☐!

        **not have/stand a cat in hell's chance** ☐!

        **not have the ghost of a chance**

have no chance at all of doing something successfully

*Linda doesn't have a hope in hell/stand a cat in hell's chance/have the ghost of a chance of winning the competition: the other competitors are much better than she is.*

**22.12**    **down on** one's **luck**

experiencing a time when one is unlucky or unfortunate

*Helen helped me when I was down on my luck — I'd just lost my job, and my wife had left me.*

**22.13**    **be on the safe side**

not take any risks, make completely sure that one will be successful

*To be on the safe side, you need to have several customers for your new product before putting it on the market.*

**22.14**    **(It's) better (to be) safe than sorry.**

It isn't worth taking any risks at all.

*That beach is dangerous, so don't go swimming there: better safe than sorry.*

**22.15**    **a fair crack of the whip**

a reasonable opportunity (given by someone) to do something

*She deserves a fair crack of the whip. Let's give her all the help we can in putting her ideas into practice.*

**22.16**    **as luck would have it**

as it was decided by chance, as it happened

*As luck would have it, we took the right turning and arrived here in good time, though we didn't really know the road.*

**22.17**    **It's a good job**

It is lucky; it is fortunate

*It's a good job you were at home when your brother phoned from Canada.*

22.18 **be just as well**

be fortunate (used about something the listener might not consider fortunate)

*It was **just as well** that you didn't know about the burglary; otherwise your holiday would have been ruined.*

22.19 **if the worst comes to the worst**

if the worst possibility happens

*If the worst comes to the worst and the weather is very bad, we can always return home from our holiday.*

22.20 **as a last resort**

as a last hope (when everything else has failed)

*I couldn't start my car and **as a last resort** I got a taxi in order to be at the office on time.*

## 23. CHOICE

23.1 **make up** one's **mind**

reach a decision

***Make up your mind** and decide which book to buy. We can't wait all day for you.*

23.2 **sit on the fence**

be uncertain which of two choices to make, be unwilling to take one side or the other in a quarrel

*Several took my side in the dispute while a few took the other side. Most of the workers, however, **sat on the fence**, waiting to see what was going to happen.*

23.3 **pick and choose**

look very carefully and choose only the best of something available

*Take the first job you can get. There's a lot of unemployment at the moment, and so no one can **pick and choose**.*

23.4 **There is nothing/little to choose between them/etc.**

It is difficult to make a choice (between two or more things) because they are so similar.

*The performance of those two cars is very similar; **there is nothing/little to choose** between them.*

23.5 **You/etc. can't have it both ways.**

You must make a choice.

***You can't have it both ways** — either you will have to pay the price or do without the goods.*

23.6 **Hobson's choice**

no choice at all

*It's **Hobson's choice**. If Ann doesn't go on holiday with her parents, she won't have any holiday at all.*

## 24. ANTICIPATION, PREPARATION

24.1 **be/stay one jump ahead of** someone

anticipate what someone will do, act before someone else does

*Our company is usually **one jump ahead of** its competitors and is almost always the first to bring out a new product.*

24.2 **set the stage/pave the way for** someone/something

prepare for someone/something, create suitable conditions for something to happen

*Frank Whittle's invention of the jet engine **set the stage for** modern air travel.*

**24.3 be all set for**

ready for, prepared for

*Bobby Lee is **all set for** his big match tonight.*

**24.4 take the words out of** someone's **mouth**

say what someone else is about to say

*I was about to say exactly what you have just said. You **took the words out of my mouth**.*

**24.5 steal** someone's **thunder**

ruin the effect of what someone was going to say or do by saying or doing it first

*Dr Fisher was about to announce a sensational cure for cancer but another doctor **stole his thunder** by announcing a similar cure first.*

**24.6 cross that bridge when** one **comes to it**

wait to see what happens before doing something, deal with a problem when it arises, and not before

*It is likely that several people on the committee will be opposed to our suggestions. But we can **cross that bridge when we come to it**.*

**24.7 Don't count your chickens before they are hatched.**

Do not anticipate some expected benefit (because it may not happen).

*I know you're expecting to make a lot of money from your invention, but **don't count your chickens before they are hatched**. People may not want to buy it.*

**24.8 in the pipeline**

being prepared or considered (for future action)

*Several suggestions are **in the pipeline** and will be considered at the next meeting.*

**24.9 in store**

ready (for someone), about to happen (to someone)

*There is a big surprise **in store** for you when you return home.*

**24.10 in for** something

about to experience something (often something unpleasant)

*The weather forecast says that we are **in for** a severe snowstorm.*

**24.11 The writing (is) on the wall**

(There are) signs of future disaster, failure, etc.

*It isn't safe for foreigners here any longer: you ought to leave. **The writing is on the wall**.*

**24.12 with bated breath**

with great anticipation (usually worry)

*I awaited the test results **with bated breath** and eventually learned that I had passed.*

**24.13 Roll on**

usually followed by a noun (e.g. summer, Christmas) to indicate that someone is greatly looking forward to the time being referred to

***Roll on** the holiday season — I do enjoy lying in bed and doing nothing.*

**24.14 play it by ear**

deal with something as it occurs

*When we get to the meeting, we'll just have to **play it by ear**. There's nothing we can do to prepare for it.*

## 25. ASSUMPTION

25.1   **take** something **for granted**
       accept that something is true without making certain, accept as normal
       something that may really be special in some way
       *You should always thank people who help you. Don't **take** their help **for granted**.*

25.2   **take** something **as read**
       assume (or accept) something without any need for further
       investigation
       *Can I **take** it **as read** that you are all familiar with the background to the matter we
       are going to discuss?*

25.3   **take** someone at **his/her word**
       **take** someone's **word for it**
       accept that what someone promises or says is true without questioning
       it in any way or making certain
       *I **took** him **at his word**, but I shouldn't have believed his promise.*
       *I **took his word for it**, but I should have checked the information myself.*

25.4   **(you can) take it from me**
       you can accept it as being true
       *You can **take it from me** that such a thing won't happen again.*

## 26. HOPES, WISHES

26.1   **keep/have** one's **fingers crossed**
       hope that everything will turn out well, hope that one will be lucky
       (people may actually cross two fingers of one hand while saying this)
       *I hope you win tonight: I'll certainly **keep my fingers crossed** for you.*

26.2   **touch/knock on wood**
       used after a remark expressing a hope for good luck (people may touch
       a piece of wood when they say this)
       *We may be lucky and get home without the car breaking down again, **touch/knock
       on wood**.*

26.3   **hope against hope**
       continue to hope for something even though it may seem very unlikely
       to happen
       *Sarah is **hoping against hope** that her parents will be alive, but the rescue party
       have not yet found any trace of survivors among the ruins.*

26.4   **pin** one's **hopes/faith on** someone/something
       hope someone (usually a single person or event) will produce the result
       one wants
       *Tom is **pinning all his hopes on** his marks in his Physics paper. Otherwise he
       won't be able to go to University as he has not done too well in the other papers.*

26.5   **(build) castles in the air**
       (have) hopes and dreams that are unlikely to be achieved
       *Paul's dreams of becoming an airline pilot are **castles in the air** as he hasn't got
       any qualifications at all.*

26.6   **(it is) wishful thinking**
       (it is) an unrealistic hope

*It is wishful thinking to imagine that the boat will return safely after the storms last week. It is long overdue already.*

26.7 **look at/see** the world/something **through rose-coloured spectacles/glasses**
have an unreasonably hopeful and cheerful attitude to something
*Tourists who visit only the attractive or wealthy parts of a city tend to **see** the city through rose-coloured spectacles/glasses.*

26.8 **with the best will in the world**
no matter how much one may wish or try to do something (good)
*With the best will in the world, one can't improve conditions in this prison because there is simply no money to do so.*

26.9 **play ball**
do something which fits in with someone else's wishes
*If he wants to do the job that way, I will **play ball** with him because I can see some advantage in his suggestions.*

26.10 **All the best!**
All my best wishes. (Often used when leaving a friend to wish him/her well)
*Well, maybe I'll see you again next week. Anyway, **all the best** for the exam!*

## 27. WANTS, DESIRES

27.1 **be dying for** something/**to do** something
want something urgently, want to do something very soon
*I'm **dying for** my lunch because I had breakfast very early.*

27.2 **would give the world for** something/**to do** something
would like something very much indeed (usually something which is unlikely to happen or not possible)
*I'd **give the world** to be able to play the piano well.*

27.3 **have** one's **heart set on** something
**set** one's **heart on** something
want something very much indeed
*Mary **has set her heart on** going to Italy for her holidays this year.*

27.4 **set** one's **sights on something**
want to have or achieve, etc.; aim for
*We have a lot of good students in the department. Most of them are **setting** their sights on well-paid and interesting jobs.*

27.5 **do one's own thing**
do what one wants to do (usually independently of any outside organisation)
*She used to work for a big company. But she gave that up because she wanted to **do her own thing** and become a writer.*

27.6 **just what the doctor ordered**
**just the job**
**just the ticket**
exactly what is needed
*This two-week holiday in Spain looks **just what the doctor ordered/just the job/just the ticket**. I think we should book it immediately.*

27.7 **can/could (well) do without**
not want
*An increase in the TV licence fee is something we **could well do without**.*

## 28. REMEMBERING

28.1 **learn/know** something **(off) by heart**
learn something, know something completely from memory
*An actor must have a good memory so that he can **learn** long speeches **off by heart**.*

28.2 **bear/keep** something **in mind**
remember something
*Please **bear in mind** that other people want to sleep at night and not listen to you practising your trumpet.*

28.3 **ring a bell**
remind someone of something, help someone to recall something
*That name **rings a bell** — I think I heard someone talking about him last year.*

28.4 have something/be **on the tip of** one's **tongue**
be on the point of remembering something (especially a name) which one has momentarily forgotten
*Her name is **on the tip of my tongue**, but I just can't recall it at the moment. No doubt it'll come back to me in a few minutes.*

## 29. FORGETTING

29.1 **slip** someone's **mind**
be forgotten by someone (used especially of something that one should have remembered to do)
*I'm sorry I didn't call to see Jane as you asked me to — it completely **slipped my mind**.*

29.2 **lose track of** someone/something
not remain informed about someone/something
*I've completely **lost track of** Ann. I haven't seen her for years and I've got no idea where she's working now.*

29.3 **lose sight of** something
forget about or ignore (especially one's original objectives)
*Doctors must be careful not to **lose sight of** the aims of their profession and think too much of its financial rewards.*

29.4 **have a memory like a sieve**
be forgetful, never remember things
*Mrs Banks **has a memory like a sieve**. She never remembers anything you tell her.*

## 30. ADMIRING, LIKING, FRIENDSHIP

30.1 **think the world of** someone/something
admire someone or something very much
*Nellie **thinks the world of** her husband and would do anything to please him.*

30.2 **think the sun shines out of** someone's **arse** [!]
admire someone very much (vulgar)
*Frank seems to **think the sun shines out of** the manager's **arse**: in his opinion, he can do no wrong.*

30.3 **paint** something **in glowing colours**
describe something in a very favourable way

*In describing his new house to me, Ted **painted it in glowing colours**. I wonder if it is really as nice as he says it is.*

30.4 **take** one's **hat off to** someone

greatly admire someone (for some action)

*I **take my hat off to** anyone who can win an argument with Mrs Thirsk.*

30.5 **fall all over** someone

show one's love or liking for someone, especially a woman

*All Tina had to do was to wear a short skirt, and men were **falling all over** her.*

30.6 **cannot take** one's **eyes off** someone/something

like someone or something very much, be very attracted to someone or something

*Robert **couldn't take his eyes off** Brenda: it was love at first sight.*

30.7 **fall/be head over heels in love**

fall/be deeply in love

*Thomas **is head over heels in love** with Belinda: he's only happy when he's with her.*

30.8 **have a crush on** someone

like someone of the opposite sex very much (used especially of immature or short-lived emotions)

*Sally **has a crush on** her English teacher, but I expect she'll get over it soon.*

30.9 **make eyes at** someone

show one's liking for someone of the opposite sex by looking at him/her with interest or admiration

*During the whole dinner, Mary's been **making eyes at** the man on the next table.*

30.10 **have eyes only for** someone/something

be very keen or interested only in someone/something (and no one/nothing else)

*Dave **had eyes only for** Ann at the party and wasn't interested in talking to anyone else.*

30.11 **gone on** someone

be very interested in or attracted to someone (beyond all reason)

*Sandra is completely **gone on** a boy in the next village and is always meeting him.*

30.12 **go/fall overboard for** someone/something

be very enthusiastic about someone/something, become very attracted to him/her/it

*The principal is very enthusiastic about the plans for a new swimming-pool at the school and seems to have **gone** completely **overboard for** them. He is even launching an appeal for extra money to build the pool.*

30.13 **have a soft spot for** someone

be fond of someone (often someone with whom one has fairly formal relations)

*I think the boss **has a soft spot for** Sylvia: she reminds him of his own daughter.*

30.14 **hit it off** (with someone)

get on well (with someone), form a good relationship (with someone)

*John and Mark **hit it off** as soon as they met. Now they're very close friends.*

30.15 **rub shoulders with**

be friendly with, meet socially

*Mr Brown **rubs shoulders with** several of the big pop stars.*

30.16 **get on like a house on fire** (with someone)
    be very good friends (with someone); enjoy someone's company
    *Helen and Annie didn't like each other at first but now they **get on like a house on fire**.*

30.17 **be on the same wavelength** (as someone)
    have the same interests and opinions (as someone), have similar feelings
    *I immediately felt that Anna was **on the same wavelength** as soon as I met her.*

30.18 **the apple of** someone's **eye**
    a person one likes more than any other, one's favourite
    *Paul is **the apple of** his father's **eye** and gets whatever he wants from him.*

30.19 **the cat's whiskers**
    something that one particularly admires or would like to have (often a machine or a device)
    *He thinks his new pocket television set is **the cat's whiskers** and is always talking about it.*

30.20 **blue-eyed boy**
    favourite person (especially of someone in a position of authority: e.g. a boss, a teacher)
    *The new clerk is the **blue-eyed boy** in this office — the manager is always praising him, whether he deserves it or not.*

30.21 **the greatest thing since sliced bread**
    something greatly admired (used in a humorous way)
    *He thinks his new calculator is **the greatest thing since sliced bread**. He's always playing with it.*

30.22 **close to** someone's **heart**
    something that someone likes very much or is very keen to encourage
    *The forming of a choir is something **close to** Mrs Flower's **heart**: she has always enjoyed singing.*

30.23 **a man/woman after** one's **own heart**
    a person whom one greatly admires (often a person who is like the speaker in some way)
    *He is **a man after my own heart**. He said exactly the things I myself would have liked to say in that situation.*

30.24 **in** someone's **good books**
    liked by someone, in favour with someone
    *Helen has been **in** her teacher's **good books** ever since she offered to carry his case.*

30.25 **let bygones be bygones**
    forget (and forgive) something done in the past
    *Why don't you stop quarrelling and become friends? Surely it's time to **let bygones be bygones**.*

## 31. POPULARITY

31.1 **in demand**
    popular, liked or wanted by a lot of people
    *He is such a popular entertainer that he is always **in demand** at local concerts.*

31.2 **be a hit with**
    be popular with

*Mike Jackson, the new pop singer, **was** certainly **a hit with** the audience at the Playhouse Theatre last night.*

31.3 **play to the gallery**
set out to win public popularity by one's performance or behaviour
*When speaking at a mass meeting, he always **plays to the gallery**. He loves popularity and tells the people only what pleases them.*

31.4 **get/climb on the bandwagon**
do something only because a lot of other people are doing it, follow popular opinion
*The president's opponents attacked him for his handling of the war, and soon all the newspapers were **climbing on the bandwagon**, publishing critical articles.*

# 32. DISLIKING

32.1 **cannot bear/stand the sight of** someone/something
dislike someone or something very much
*I **cannot stand the sight of** a garden not properly cared for: it looks so untidy.*

32.2 **not/be someone's cup of tea**
not be what someone likes
*He **isn't my cup of tea**. I've never spoken much to him, but I find his attitude unpleasant.*

32.3 **have a thing about** something
dislike something very much (used also to indicate a strong liking for someone or something)
*I **have a thing about** dirty paper money — I don't even like touching it.*
*She **has a thing about** men with beards. All three of her husbands had long beards!*

32.4 **have a down on** someone
dislike someone (and treat him/her unfairly)
*I am sure my employer **has a down on** me: he always gives me the most unpleasant tasks to do.*

32.5 **hate** someone's **guts** [!]
dislike a person very much indeed
*He's the most unpleasant person I've ever met. I **hate his guts**.*

32.6 **hate** someone/something **like poison**
dislike someone or something very much
*I never drink whisky: in fact, I **hate it like poison**.*

32.7 **not have a lot of time** for someone/something
dislike, have a low opinion of someone/something
*Alexei Sayle **doesn't have a lot of time** for TV interviewers: he thinks they always ask silly questions.*

32.8 **sick to the (back) teeth of/fed up to the (back) teeth with/of** [!]
angry, tired and disgusted with someone/something
*I'm **sick to the back teeth of** people who do nothing but criticise.*

32.9 **give** one **the creeps** [!]
arouse one's dislike or fear
*This house **gives me the creeps**. It's the kind of place where you'd expect to see a ghost.*

32.10  **There's no love lost between** them
They dislike each other
*There's no love lost between Joe and his uncle: they won't even speak to each other.*

32.11  someone's **name is mud/dirt**
someone is very much disliked (or not in favour).
*He had broken so many promises to his colleagues that his **name was mud** in the office.*

32.12  **in** someone's **bad/black books**
disliked by someone, out of favour with them
*Annie's been **in** the teacher's **bad books** ever since he caught her drawing a picture of him on the blackboard.*

32.13  **have mixed feelings** about someone/something
like in some ways and dislike in others
*She **has mixed feelings** about her husband's parents — she likes them in some ways but not in others.*

32.14  **wouldn't be seen dead** doing something
feel that one would be deeply ashamed if one did something
*I **wouldn't be seen dead** in that nightclub — it has a very bad reputation.*

32.15  **sour grapes**
used when someone pretends to dislike something which he really wants, but cannot have
*Tim says my new car isn't very good, but I think it's a case of **sour grapes**. He's always wanted a car himself.*

## 33. DISAPPROVAL

33.1  **take a dim view of** someone/something
disapprove of someone/something
*Mrs Long **took a dim view of** the two guests who did not arrive in time for the meal she had cooked.*

33.2  **give** someone **the bird**
show disapproval of someone, especially an actor, singer, etc. (used about an audience)
*The comedian **got the bird** from the audience, who clearly disapproved of his act from the beginning.*

33.3  **not quite the thing**
not acceptable, too old-fashioned
*It's **not quite the thing** to wear tight trousers. They've gone out of fashion.*

33.4  **in bad odour with** someone
disapproved of, thought badly of (used about people)
*That shopkeeper is **in bad odour with** several of his customers, as he has not delivered the goods they ordered.*

## 34. REJECTION

34.1  **give** someone **the brush-off/cold shoulder**
reject someone (especially a member of the opposite sex)
*Tina **gave** John **the brush-off** and refused to go to the concert with him.*

34.2 **fall on deaf ears**
be rejected or disregarded (used especially of requests for help, etc.)
*The employees' request for an increase in wages **fell on deaf ears**, and they received no increase at all.*

34.3 **be kicked in the teeth/be given a kick in the teeth**
be unexpectedly rejected or discouraged
*He felt as though he had **been kicked in the teeth** when he was dismissed after he had worked so hard for the company.*

34.4 **have nothing to do with** someone/something
refuse to have any connection with someone/something
*Mary will have **nothing to do with** me since her father quarrelled with mine. She won't even speak to me.*

34.5 **Beat it!/Hop it** !
Go away !
***Beat it!/Hop it!** I am tired of arguing with you.*


# 35. SCORN, SARCASM

35.1 **look down** one's **nose** at someone/something
scorn someone or something
*She always **looked down her nose** at her neighbours and thought she was much better than they were.*

35.2 **turn up** one's **nose** at something
scorn something, reject it because it is not good enough
*Mary **turned her nose up** at the plastic roses she was given. She wanted real ones.*

35.3 **(give** someone) **a smack in the eye**
(give) a severe blow to someone's feelings or to someone's pride
*Mr Shaw tried to speak at the conference, but the chairman told him to be quiet and sit down. It was a real **smack in the eye** for him.*

35.4 **take the mickey (out** of someone)
make fun of someone, humiliate someone through sarcasm, etc.
*Stanley does not like Eric and he **took the mickey** out of him by imitating his manner of speech.*

35.5 **have no time for** someone/something
scorn someone or something, not want to waste one's time on someone or something
*Mr Smart **had no time for** any idle workmen. All his men were well paid and he expected them to work hard.*

35.6 **Big deal!/Big thrill!/So what!** !
used to show scorn about something that has just been said
*"Tommy got a home computer for his birthday." "**Big deal!/Big thrill!/So what!** Some other children in the class have had home computers for years!"*

35.7 **Says you** !
So you say. (used to show one's scorn and disbelief)
*You're going to make a million pounds in this deal? **Says you!** Only a fool would believe that.*

## 36. REFUSAL

36.1    **give someone (the) first refusal**
allow someone the first chance to obtain or refuse something (before offering it to anyone else)
*He wants to buy my house and I told him I would **give him first refusal** before offering it to anyone else.*

36.2    **Nothing doing.**
**No way.**
**not for all the tea in China**
**not for love (n)or money**
Certainly not (used to show emphatic refusal)
*1. **No way.**/**Nothing doing.** I shan't put money into a scheme that has no chance of success.*
*2. I wouldn't go in his car **for all the tea in China**/**for love (n)or money**. He's such a dangerous driver.*

## 37. ACCEPTANCE, BELIEF

37.1    **rise to the bait/swallow the bait**
be tricked (by something said or offered) into doing what someone wants to do
*Susan wanted to make John angry, and when she insulted him, he **rose to the bait** and lost his temper.*

37.2    **fall for/swallow** something **hook, line and sinker**
accept or believe something completely
*He **fell for** the beggar's story **hook, line and sinker** and gave him all the money he had in his wallet.*

37.3    **take** something **lying down**
accept something bad without complaining
*Mr Johnson had to **take** the criticism of his work **lying down** because he did not want to risk losing his job.*

37.4    **stick in** someone's **throat/gullet**
be hard for someone to accept
*The idea of contributing money to this scheme **sticks in my throat/gullet** as I don't agree with its objectives.*

37.5    **come to terms with** something
accept something usually unpleasant or difficult (and start to deal with it)
*It was a great shock to him when he was dismissed from his job. He's only just **coming to terms with** the situation.*

## 38. COMPLAINT

38.1    **have a bone to pick with** someone
have a reason to complain or argue about something with someone
*I **have a bone to pick with** you. What did you mean by saying that I am untidy in my habits?*

38.2    **kick up a fuss/row**
complain (violently), cause a disturbance

*If I were you, I wouldn't kick up a fuss/row over that decision. There's no chance of getting it changed now.*

38.3 **take** someone **to task**

complain to someone (about something he has done), criticise someone

*He took me to task over the way I repaired the roof of his house and said the work was not satisfactory.*

38.4 **no joke/beyond a joke**

too serious to laugh about (often used to indicate the seriousness of a complaint)

*I know we used to laugh at the things he did, but now it's getting beyond a joke. He's becoming really annoying.*

## 39. CRITICISM

39.1 **tear/pull** someone/something **to pieces**

criticise very harshly

*His criticism of the factory was very harsh and he tore the manager to pieces over it.*

39.2 **tear a strip off** someone/**tear strips off** someone

criticise someone, speak very severely to someone

*The football manager was so annoyed at the lack of initiative shown by his team that he tore a strip off them during the interval. As a result, they played a lot better in the second half of the match.*

39.3 **put** someone **on the carpet**

speak severely to someone about something he/she has done

*The directors of the company put the manager on the carpet because production had fallen so low.*

39.4 **give** someone **what for**

say hard and angry words to someone

*I'll give you what for if you don't tidy your room.*

39.5 **tell** someone **where to get off**

speak angrily to someone because of his/her bad behaviour, rudeness, etc.

*The boss wanted me to work an extra three hours without pay, but I told him where to get off.*

39.6 **come under fire**

be criticised

*James came under fire in the office after he wrote a very critical article in the company magazine.*

39.7 **not pull** one's **punches**

not criticise someone/something as much as one could (often used in the negative)

*Come now, give me your honest opinion of Henry. Don't pull any punches.*

39.8 **the pot calling the kettle black**

used about a speaker who criticises someone else for faults which he has himself

*Why should you blame Henry for drinking too much? You drink too much yourself. It's a case of the pot calling the kettle black.*

## 40. PRAISE

40.1 **praise to the skies**
praise very highly
*When the novel was first published, all the critics **praised** it **to the skies**. They said it was a wonderful piece of writing.*

40.2 **sing** someone's/something's **praises**
praise someone/something (often to more than one person)
*His wife is an extremely good cook, and he is always **singing her praises** for the meals she prepares.*

40.3 **blow** one's **own trumpet**
praise oneself, boast (used in a derogatory way)
*Jim is very good at **blowing his own trumpet**: to listen to him, one would think he was the only man who could do the job.*

40.4 **give** someone **full marks for** something
used to praise someone for something or to express admiration
*The newspapers **gave** the Prime Minister **full marks for** the way he handled the difficult talks on trade with Japan.*

## 41. RIGHT

41.1 **start off on the right foot**
Opposite: **start off on the wrong foot**
do something well at the beginning
*I **started off on the right foot** in my new job and the manager seemed very pleased.*

41.2 **spot on**
exactly right
*"What's the population of that country?"*
*"2.3 million."*
*"That's right. You're **spot on**."*

41.3 **on the right track**
proceeding correctly, moving in the right direction
*I think we are **on the right track** in our research. But we can't be sure until results start coming in next year.*

41.4 **with a clean slate**
with any previous mistakes ignored or unrecorded
*I'm not interested in hearing about any mistakes you made in your previous job. Now you've joined our company, you can start off **with a clean slate**.*

41.5 **wipe the slate clean**
forget about past mistakes and faults
*Let's **wipe the slate clean** and ignore the mistakes he has made in the past: I'm sure this will encourage him in his future behaviour.*

41.6 **set/put the record straight**
correct something (usually a belief about some past event)
*I'm trying to **set the record straight** about my brother: he was truly innocent of the crime.*

41.7 **put** one's **own house in order**
put things right in one's own affairs
*The teachers at the school should **put their own house in order** before they start blaming parents for the pupils' behaviour.*

## 42. WRONG

42.1 **get hold of the wrong end of the stick**
completely misunderstand something
*That's not what the lecturer said at all — you've **got hold of the wrong end of the stick** and you obviously don't understand the points that he made.*

42.2 **up to no good**
doing or planning to do something bad
*Those three men outside the bank are clearly **up to no good**. They look as if they may be planning a robbery.*

42.3 **drop a brick/clanger**
make a mistake which causes embarrassment
*I **dropped a clanger** when I told Mary I had seen her husband at the party. She thought he'd been working late at the office!*

42.4 **bark up the wrong tree**
be mistaken, have a wrong idea about something
*You're **barking up the wrong tree**. I didn't take your book: it was Marion who borrowed it.*

42.5 **wide of the mark**
wrong, incorrect (often used for a guess or prediction)
*Our forecast of the demand for the new book was very **wide of the mark**: we have sold far more than we expected.*

42.6 **wise after the event**
knowing what one should have done after something has happened (when it is too late)
*Our house has been broken into; we should have installed a burglar alarm, but it is easy to be **wise after the event**.*

42.7 **fall guy** [!]
someone who is easily tricked and can be blamed if anything goes wrong
*It looks as if I'm the person who will be blamed if the plan fails. I'm the **fall guy**.*

## 43. GOOD

43.1 **a man/woman/boy/girl/etc. in a million**
someone who is the best or very special in a certain way
*Harry's wife is **a woman in a million**. She's attractive, intelligent and devoted to her husband.*

43.2 **the last word**
the best example, the most recent model, etc.
*This is **the last word** in tennis racquets and is made to the highest standards. All the world's top tennis stars are using this model now.*

43.3 **second to none**
as good as (or better than) any other
*The new leader is a man whose reputation is **second to none**.*

43.4 **the salt of the earth**
a person or people who are very good, reliable and honest
*The people in the village are **the salt of the earth**. You can always depend on them.*

43.5  **of the first water/magnitude/order**
of the highest, best, worst, etc. quality
*He is a rascal **of the first order**: he'd even cheat his own mother if he could.*

43.6  **a cut above the rest**
better than the others
*The new leader of the trade union is certainly **a cut above the rest**.*

43.7  **made to measure**
perfectly suitable
*Here is a table which is **made to measure** for our kitchen: it's exactly the right shape and colour. It's just what I want.*

43.8  **done/cooked to a turn**
perfectly cooked (used about food)
*This steak is marvellous: it's **done to a turn**!*

43.9  **up to scratch**
reaching the required standard
*Your work is not **up to scratch**. If you don't improve, you'll lose your job.*

43.10  **put up a good show**
do well (especially in some difficult situation, contest, etc.)
*Although Rocky didn't win, he certainly **put up a good show**.*

43.11  **do** someone **proud**
treat someone extremely well
*Mr and Mrs Thompson always **do us proud** whenever we go to have a meal with them — the food is always excellent.*

43.12  **turn up trumps**
do something surprisingly well, often at the last moment
*The leading actor fell ill a week before the play, but Frank **turned up trumps**. He took on the part at the last minute and made an excellent job of it.*

43.13  **a saving grace**
a good feature that keeps someone/something from being completely bad
*The cinema, though very small and uncomfortable, has at least one **saving grace**: it always shows very good films.*

43.14  **go from strength to strength**
get constantly better, be more and more successful
*Linda Harvey started as a singer in a local group, but since then she's **gone from strength to strength**. Now she's a big star and travels all over the world.*

## 44. BAD, POOR IN QUALITY

44.1  **a dead loss**
someone/something that is completely bad, hopeless, useless, etc.
*I shouldn't have asked Dave to help me with the decorating. He's **a dead loss**. He can't do anything practical.*

44.2  **a bad egg**
a worthless person
*Henry Higginson's **a bad egg**. If he wants to borrow any money from you, don't lend it to him.*

44.3  **a bad/rotten apple**
a weak or worthless person in an otherwise good group of people

*There are just one or two **rotten apples** in the police force – men who are dishonest and corrupt.*

44.4 **Achilles' heel**

a weak point or fault in someone or something (that is otherwise very good)

*On the whole, Ernest was a good man but his **Achilles' heel** was his violent temper.*

44.5 **a nasty piece of work**

a very unpleasant person

*Joe Hanson's **a nasty piece of work**. Everything he does is to his own advantage.*

44.6 **no great shakes**

not very effective, of poor quality

*As Prime Minister, he was **no great shakes**. He never did anything worthwhile during his whole period of office.*

44.7 **not too/so hot**

not very good

*"Do you like your new television?" "No, I don't. The picture's very poor and the sound's **not so hot** either."*

44.8 **not be all it/he/she/etc. is cracked up to be**

not be as good as people say it/he/she is

*The course on photography **isn't** really **all it is cracked up to be**. The lecturer isn't a good photographer himself.*

44.9 **on the blink**

not working properly (usually used about something electric)

*"Did you see the play on TV last night?" "No, I didn't. My TV is **on the blink** at the moment."*

44.10 **go haywire**

stop working properly, go out of control

*Oh dear! This tape-recorder has **gone haywire**. I can't re-wind it.*

44.11 **far gone**

in a bad state, near a state of ruin, collapse or death

*That chair is too **far gone** to repair: the frame is broken in several places.*

44.12 **tarred with the same brush**

thought to have the same faults (as someone else)

*Harold and his brother are both **tarred with the same brush**. People say they both spend too much time drinking.*

44.13 **scrape the bottom of the barrel**

use the worst people or things because no others are left

*The History Department seems to be **scraping the bottom of the barrel** with the new students. All the good students have entered the Medical Faculty.*

44.14 **not be as black as he/she/it is painted**

not be as bad as people say

*People say he's a heavy gambler but he's **not as black as he's painted**. He usually stops before he loses too much money.*

44.15 **a black sheep**

someone who is bad and brings shame on his/her family or community

*Henry was always **the black sheep** of the family. He was lazy and dishonest, and eventually ran away from home.*

44.16  **make a pig's ear out of** something
      do something badly and leave a mess behind one
      *You've **made a pig's ear out of** cutting that hedge. It looks terrible now, and you've left branches all over the ground.*

44.17  **wash** one's **dirty linen in public**
      talk in public about one's private quarrels or the faults of one's own group
      *Don't **wash your dirty linen in public**, and stop talking about your family quarrels.*

## 45. VALUE, WORTH

45.1  **worth** one's/it's **weight in gold**
      very valuable indeed
      *I find this book **worth its weight in gold**. I couldn't possibly understand anything at all about the subject without it.*

45.2  **worth** one's **salt**
      deserving admiration, deserving the money that one is paid
      *He's made an excellent job of everything he's done in the company. He's certainly **worth his salt**.*

45.3  **do justice to** someone/something
      treat or speak of someone/something with the respect deserved
      *I don't care for Bert, but **to do him justice** he's very hardworking.*

45.4  **worth** someone's **while**
      profitable for someone
      *It would be **worth** your **while** to buy Bob's car – he's asking an incredibly low price for it.*

45.5  **a golden handshake**
      a large payment when someone leaves a company
      *Did you hear that the firm gave Mr Smith **a golden handshake** of £50,000 when he left last month?*

45.6  a/someone's **nest egg**
      money which has been saved for use in the future
      *If you save £10 a week, you'll have a nice little **nest egg** when you retire.*

45.7  **pay through the nose**
      pay far too much for something
      *I found I had **paid through the nose** for my new curtains. I could have bought them much cheaper at Universal Stores.*

45.8  **(sweet) Fanny Adams** !
      nothing at all (usually used in a vulgar or offensive way)
      *I thought this ring was diamond, but it's made of glass — so it's worth **sweet Fanny Adams!***

45.9  **chicken feed**
      a very small amount of money, something unimportant
      *One pound was a lot of money at one time, but it's **chicken feed** today. It won't even buy a meal now!*

45.10  **good-for-nothing**
      worthless (used chiefly about a person)
      *John is a **good-for-nothing**. He's very lazy and I don't think he's honest.*

45.11 **count for nothing**
be worthless, not be treated as important
*He never keeps any promises he makes. His word counts for nothing.*

## 46. USEFUL

46.1 **come in handy**
prove useful
*These old boxes may come in handy some time. We can always store things in them.*

46.2 **stand** someone **in good stead**
be useful or helpful (to someone) in time of need
*The experience I have gained should stand me in good stead in my new job.*

## 47. USELESS

47.1 **dead wood**
someone/something that is no longer necessary or useful
*We really must cut out the dead wood in the office. We have too many clerks who seem to sleep most of the day.*

47.2 **a bad lot**
a useless or bad person
*He's a bad lot — he's spent longer in prison than he's spent working.*

47.3 **a white elephant**
something that costs a lot but is worthless or useless
*The new opera house will be a white elephant: it is too small for proper opera productions, and no large opera company will want to use it.*

47.4 **a fool's errand**
a useless journey or task
*The people who advised to come to me for money sent you on a fool's errand. I never lend money.*

47.5 **a wild goose chase**
a useless search, a chase with no chance of success
*It's a wild goose chase looking for spare parts for my car. There just aren't any available now.*

## 48. SUITABLE

48.1 **(right/just) up** someone's **street**
exactly suitable for someone, just what someone is interested in
*It's quite a coincidence you asked me about old steam engines. I'm very interested in that subject — it's just up my street.*

48.2 **in** one's **element**
in a situation suited to one's character or abilities
*Look at Harry on that motorbike. He's in his element: he loves anything on two wheels!*

48.3 **(in)** one's **line of country**
the kind of thing one can do well, understands or likes
*She is fluent in French, and very keen on French writers. So this course in French literature will be just her line of country.*

48.4 **be cut out for**
be naturally suited for (often used in the negative)
*He seems to **be cut out for** the job because of his wide experience and success in similar jobs.*

48.5 **fit/fill the bill**
be very suitable, meet all the requirements
*That table will **fit the bill** admirably as it will match all the other furniture in the room.*

48.6 **strike while the iron's hot**
do something in time, while a suitable moment is still present
*We must **strike while the iron's hot** and get Mr Tibbits to sign the agreement before he changes his mind.*

## 49. UNSUITABLE

49.1 **stick out like a sore thumb**
seem very unsuitable, out of place
*That tall new building in the market square **sticks out like a sore thumb** among all the old shops around it.*

49.2 **a square peg in a round hole**
a person who does not fit in
*They gave one of their mechanics a job in the office, but he doesn't like it. He is **a square peg in a round hole**.*

49.3 **like a fish out of water**
out of place, unsuitable for the situation
*I felt **like a fish out of water** at the meeting of astronomers as I knew so little about the subject.*

## 50. IMPORTANT

50.1 **the be-all and end-all**
the most important goal or aim
*There's more to life than simply making a lot of money — money isn't **the be-all and end-all** of life.*

50.2 **be/mean (all) the world to**
be very important to
*Dave loves his wife very much: she **means all the world to** him.*

50.3 **a must**
something necessary, something very important
*Our flat is such a long way from the office that a car is **a must**. There are no bus services at all!*

50.4 **the long and (the) short of it**
the most important fact (stated briefly)
***The long and short of it** is that Timothy is not good enough to play in his school football team.*

50.5 **the bare bones**
the essential or most important parts of something (usually facts)
*I only know **the bare bones** of his proposal. No doubt he will tell me more next time I see him.*

**50.6  a/the golden rule**
*very important principle or rule*
*The golden rule in any ballgame is to keep your eye on the ball.*

**50.7  the big guns**
the important people in an organisation (used only in the plural)
*"I hear that the big guns from London will be visiting the office next week."*
*"Exactly who will be coming?"*
*"The chairman, the secretary and the general manager."*

**50.8  in high places**
in important positions (of authority)
*Mr Small may be able to help us. At least, he knows one or two people in high places.*

**50.9  a big fish in a small pond**
an important person in a small community
*The headmaster of the village school did not want to be promoted to a big school in the city. He preferred to be a big fish in a small pond.*

**50.10  the top brass**
high-ranking officers or officials (chiefly used in connection with the army, navy and air force)
*The army college was visited by all the top brass, including the general himself.*

**50.11  a/the leading light**
an important person in a group
*She is the leading light in the local dramatic society and always has the main part in their plays.*

**50.12  (the) top dog**
the person in control, the most important or powerful person
*Terry likes to be top dog wherever he goes: he ought to learn to let others have a little more power.*

**50.13  a/the big cheese/shot/noise**
a/the most important, a most powerful person
*You'd better listen to him. He's a big shot in this company, and people usually do what he says.*

**50.14  pride of place**
most important position
*This cup I have just won will take pride of place in my living-room. I'm very proud of it.*

**50.15  a/the high spot**
the most important part of an event
*The high spot of the school concert was the performance by the youngest children. They sang very well indeed.*

**50.16  the big time** ⚠
the top level in sport or entertainment
*He's in the big time now: he plays football for one of the most important clubs.*

**50.17  the 64,000 dollar question**
the key question, the most important question
*Now we have the 64,000 dollar question. Who is going to win the election next week?*

50.18  **get down to brass tacks**
>       begin to talk about the important facts in a situation
>       *We have talked about replacing this machine for a long time, but we must now **get down to brass tacks** and decide what type to buy.*

50.19  **make a meal (out) of** something
>       treat something as more important than it really is
>       *I don't really think the question is all that important: I don't want to **make a meal of** it when I address the meeting.*

50.20  **the red carpet (treatment)**
>       special ceremonies (or respect in general) given to welcome someone important
>       *The government minister was given **the red carpet treatment** when he came to open the new university.*

50.21  **when the chips are down**
>       **when it comes to the crunch**
>       when a situation is really important or a choice must be made
>       *Harold complains quite a lot, but **when the chips are down** he always defends his company and is really very loyal.*

50.22  **the name of the game** [!]
>       the main idea in something, what something is all about
>       *In most sports, **the name of the game** is concentration. You'll never win without it.*


## 51. UNIMPORTANT

51.1  **a cog in the wheel/machine**
>       someone with an unimportant part in a large organisation or plan
>       *Although John thinks he has an important job, he is really only **a cog in the wheel**. The company is very big, and he is responsible for only one small department.*

51.2  **nothing to write home about**
>       something that is not very important, interesting or effective
>       *The food in the hotel was **nothing to write home about**. It was never very interesting.*

51.3  **neither here nor there**
>       unimportant, making no difference to a situation (especially an unimportant fact or choice)
>       *Whether we change the first sentence in the proposal is **neither here nor there**. The important point is whether we agree with the proposal.*

51.4  **take a back seat**
>       take a position of less importance
>       *He had to **take a back seat** because of ill health. He resigned from his position as chairman of the committee and became just an ordinary member.*

51.5  **play second fiddle to** someone
>       have a less important position than someone else
>       *William has now taken control of the sales department. John used to be in charge but was not very successful and is now having to **play second fiddle to** William.*

51.6  **a dead duck**
>       a subject or plan which is no longer worth considering
>       *The plan for installing the new machine is **a dead duck**. We are no longer making that type of product.*

**51.7**   **split hairs**

argue about unimportant detail

*"So, your cousin is coming to visit us?" "She isn't my cousin. She's my mother's cousin." "Well, let's not **split hairs**. The important thing is that she's coming."*

**51.8**   **a storm in a teacup**

a fierce argument about something unimportant

*The argument about the type of shelves to install in the library was only **a storm in a teacup** and has now been forgotten.*

**51.9**   **make a mountain out of a molehill**

exaggerate the importance of something (usually a small difficulty)

*Arriving five minutes late was not the disaster you think it was. Stop **making a mountain out of a molehill**.*

**51.10**   **make light of** something

treat something serious or worrying as unimportant

*Betty **made light of** her illness, which was more serious than she admitted.*

**51.11**   **not (be able to) see the wood for the trees**

be so concerned with a large number of small details that one does not notice the important facts

*The offer which the government made on atomic weapons was very complex. Many people did not understand its importance at first because they could **not see the wood for the trees**.*

## 52. ORDINARY, AVERAGE

**52.1**   **middle-of-the-road**

average, ordinary

*Joe is adopting a **middle-of-the-road** approach to this proposal — he's neither opposed to it nor very much in favour of it.*

**52.2**   **run-of-the-mill**

average, ordinary, not particularly good or interesting

*The pianist gave a **run-of-the-mill** performance of the concerto, with no features of special interest.*

**52.3**   **the man in the street**

the ordinary person

*In my opinion, **the man in the street** is more interested in good football than in good music.*

**52.4**   **the rank and file**

the ordinary members of an organisation

*The new company has highly trained supervisors but **the rank and file** of the employees have no special qualifications.*

**52.5**   **the grass roots**

the ordinary people in an organisation, a country, etc.

*The government has abolished the death penalty but there is still much support for it at **the grass roots**, among ordinary people.*

**52.6**   **the boy next door**

an ordinary boy

*The film-star was successful because he always seemed to be **the boy next door** — ordinary, friendly and very likeable.*

52.7   **any/every Tom, Dick and/or Harry**
       anyone at all (no matter who he/she is)
       *You have to be a special person to join the club — they certainly don't let **any Tom, Dick or Harry** become a member.*


# 53. EXTRAORDINARY, UNIQUE

53.1   **out of this world**
       wonderful, unique, excellent
       *Sylvia, your cooking is **out of this world**. What a wonderful meal we have just had!*

53.2   **a red-letter day**
       a very special occasion
       *Next Saturday will be **a red-letter day** for me. My brother's coming home from the army.*

53.3   **a flash in the pan**
       something that is suddenly and briefly successful (and unlikely to happen again)
       *Our football team has begun the new season very well. However, it's probably just **a flash in the pan** — I expect we'll end up at the bottom of the league, as usual.*


# 54. FAIRNESS

54.1   **play the game**
       do something fairly and honourably
       *Harry should **play the game** and take the children to the cinema as he promised to do.*

54.2   **give the devil his due**
       be fair in praising someone even though one may not like that person
       *I don't like the man, but to **give the devil his due**, he really is a splendid guitarist.*

54.3   **have to hand it to** someone
       be forced to admit someone's good qualities, etc.
       *Janet isn't very reliable, but I **have to hand it to** her: she always works very hard.*

54.4   **Fair do's**
       Be fair
       ***Fair do's**. I helped you: now you help me, please.*


# 55. UNFAIRNESS

55.1   **(with) no holds barred**
       without restrictions or rules, with anything allowed (however unfair)
       *There will be **no holds barred** at the next election, and candidates will make personal attacks on each other in their speeches.*

55.2   **catch 22/Catch 22**
       an unfair rule designed to prevent anyone from getting out of a certain situation
       *This is a **Catch 22** situation. I can't get a visa unless I have an air-ticket, and I can't get an air-ticket unless I first have a visa!*

55.3 **hard done by**
    unfairly treated
    *I felt **hard done by** as I didn't receive the salary I had been promised.*

## 56. INNOCENCE

56.1 **clear** someone's **name**
    prove someone's innocence
    *My son was not guilty of the offence for which he was convicted. I will do everything possible to **clear his name**.*

56.2 **give** someone **the benefit of the doubt**
    judge someone as innocent, etc. even if one cannot be certain
    *We don't know whether he is telling the truth but I think we should **give him the benefit of the doubt**, as his past record is good.*

## 57. GUILT

57.1 **catch** someone **red-handed**
    discover a person while he is in the act of doing something wrong or unlawful
    *The police **caught** the burglar **red-handed** as he was climbing into the house through the window.*

## 58. HONESTY, TRUST, LOYALTY

58.1 **fair and square**
    in an honest way, without any possibility of argument
    *Sonia won the final **fair and square**. There is no doubt at all that she was much better than her opponent.*

58.2 **above board**
    honest, not secret
    *The proceedings of the committee were all **above board**: anyone who wished could attend, and no facts were hidden.*

58.3 **on the level**
    truthful(ly), honest(ly)
    *Fred Champion's **on the level**. He'll do a proper job for you and charge you a reasonable price.*

58.4 **as straight as a die**
    completely honest
    *If she says she spent that amount of money on hotel expenses, then she's telling the truth. She is **as straight as a die**.*

58.5 **honest to God/goodness** !
    truthfully
    *The car's in excellent condition, **honest to God**. If you buy it, you won't have any trouble with it.*

58.6 **a man of his word**
    a trustworthy or honest man who keeps his promises
    *Dr Lee is **a man of his word**. If he promises to do anything, he'll do it.*

**58.7   the straight and narrow (path)**
a good and honest way of living
*Vince used to drink too much, but now that he's married, he's keeping to **the straight and narrow**.*

**58.8   go straight**
lead an honest life (after being convicted of a crime), not break the law again
*When Harry was released from prison, he promised to **go straight** and keep out of trouble.*

**58.9   make no bones about something**
speak firmly and frankly about something
*I'll **make no bones about** it — I don't think you did a good job of painting my house.*

**58.10   not to put too fine a point on it**
speaking (to you) clearly and honestly
***Not to put too fine a point on it**, I find it hard to believe your story. Are you sure it's true?*

**58.11   call a spade a spade**
speak frankly (and possibly impolitely), talk about things as they really are
*She speaks very frankly to everyone and is not afraid to **call a spade a spade**, even with her boss.*

**58.12   speak one's own mind**
speak frankly, say what one really thinks
*I'm going to **speak my mind**. Briefly, your behaviour at the party was disgraceful.*

**58.13   give it to someone straight**
speak frankly to someone, without softening the truth in any way
*I'll **give it to** you **straight**: I'm fed up of listening to your complaints.*

**58.14   straight out**
directly, without hesitation (used of someone speaking)
*Mary told me **straight out** that she was fed up and wanted to leave.*

**58.15   come clean**
confess, tell the whole truth (especially after lying)
***Come clean**: you have told me only part of the truth so far. Now tell me everything.*

**58.16   make a clean breast of something**
make a full confession of something
*"Come on. **Make a clean breast of** it. It was you who stole the camera, wasn't it?"*

# 59. DECEIT, DISTRUST, DISLOYALTY

**59.1   a snake in the grass**
someone who cannot be trusted and may be dangerous (used in a derogatory way)
*Alan's **a snake in the grass**. He'll tell you he's going to do one thing and then he'll do something nasty instead.*

**59.2** **a stab in the back**

an attack from someone whom one thinks of as a friend

*I was very hurt when Jane made those stupid remarks about me. I had not expected a stab in the back from her.*

**59.3** **do the dirty on** someone

cheat or treat someone unfairly (especially someone one knows personally)

*He did the dirty on me by selling me a radio that was broken. I'm sure he knew that it wasn't working properly.*

**59.4** **sell** someone/something **down the river**

betray someone/something

*We've been sold down the river! Our leaders have made an agreement with the bosses, and it doesn't give us any of the things we wanted.*

**59.5** **take** someone **for a ride**

deceive, trick, cheat someone

*The man who sold me this camera took me for a ride. It's nowhere near as good as he said it was.*

**59.6** **pull a fast one on** someone

deceive or cheat someone

*He tried to pull a fast one on me by selling me some stolen goods.*

**59.7** **pull the wool over** someone's **eyes**

deceive someone, hide facts which someone should know

*Dave never told them that the goods he was trying to sell were faulty. I think he was trying to pull the wool over their eyes.*

**59.8** **shoot a line** $\boxed{!}$

tell lies about oneself, boast untruthfully

*Stop shooting a line. You were never in the army, were you?*

**59.9** **play fast and loose**

behave deceitfully and selfishly

*Mike's playing fast and loose with Sarah. She never knows whether their engagement is on or off.*

**59.10** **lead** someone **up the garden path**

trick someone into believing something false

*Amanda spent a lot of time looking for a house when Freddie asked her to marry him. But now she realises he was leading her up the garden path and never really intended to marry her.*

**59.11** **pull** someone's **leg**

make fun of someone by deceiving them

*You shouldn't have believed me when I said someone had crashed into your new car. I was only pulling your leg.*

**59.12** **sail under false colours**

deceive people by pretending to be different from the person one is (or to have something which one does not have)

*The candidate for the job was sailing under false colours by claiming to have experience which he did not really have.*

**59.13** **not born yesterday**

not easily deceived

*Surely you don't expect me to believe you! I wasn't born yesterday.*

**59.14  wheeling and dealing**

bargaining or doing business in a clever (and sometimes dishonest) way

*He is well-known for his **wheeling and dealing**. When he bargains with you, he usually has already made a bargain with someone else.*

**59.15  cook the books**

make false records (especially business accounts) in order to take money unlawfully

*The cashier **cooked the books** by making false entries so that no one would notice the £500 he had taken.*

**59.16  line** one's **own pockets**

make a lot of money dishonestly

*One of the salesmen has been **lining his own pockets** by not paying the company all the money he collected from the orders.*

**59.17  grease/oil** someone's **palm**

bribe someone to do something dishonest

*Surely you don't expect me to **grease your palm** in order to let my cousin pass the test?*

**59.18  live by/on** one's **wits**

earn money by whatever means possible (especially in a cunning or even dishonest way)

*No one knows what he does to earn a living: he must **live on** his **wits**.*

**59.19  sail close to the wind**

do or say something which is almost dishonest or illegal

*I don't wish to deal with him. He sails far too **close to the wind** and some of his business methods are almost illegal.*

**59.20  a blacklist**

a list of people or organisations regarded as untrustworthy, etc.

*Most companies have **a blacklist** of untrustworthy people with whom they refuse to deal.*

**59.21  a tall story**

something difficult to believe

*Surely you didn't walk all the way to Rome from Paris. That's **a tall story**.*

**59.22  a white lie**

a kind untruth (i.e. not a serious lie but something untrue said to avoid hurting someone)

*When John asked me if I liked his new tie, I told **a white lie** and said how attractive it was. But really it looked terrible!*

## 60. AUTHORITY, POWER

**60.1  rule the roost**

be the most powerful person in a group, be in charge of the group

*John **rules the roost** at home: his children and even his wife do everything he says.*

**60.2  call the tune**

decide what should be done, have control over events

*Mr Lowe is paying for the project, and so he **calls the tune**. Consequently, we all try to do things the way he wants.*

**60.3** **lay down the law**
give orders which must be obeyed, give commands forcefully (often used in a derogatory way)
*Mrs Sheraton laid down the law and insisted that her nephew and niece returned home by nine o'clock each night — even though they were both over 18!*

**60.4** **call the shots**
decide what should be done
*The manager should be calling the shots but in fact the workers are in a very powerful position at the moment.*

**60.5** **take** someone/something **in hand**
take control of someone/something
*Please take James in hand and tell him not to be so rude.*

**60.6** **have the upper/whip hand**
be in control or power
*Helen has the whip hand in her department and will not allow anyone to interfere.*

**60.7** **keep a tight rein on**
keep strict control over
*The manager kept a tight rein on the staff, making sure they did not leave even a minute early each day.*

**60.8** **take a tough line with**
be strict with, be firm in dealing with
*There is a need for the police to take a tough line with football hooligans.*

**60.9** **rule** (a country/people/etc.) **with a rod of iron**
control (a country/people/etc.) very strictly
*The new president ruled with a rod of iron and had all his opponents arrested.*

**60.10** **come the heavy hand**
try to force someone to do something (often used in negative imperatives)
*Don't come the heavy hand with me. If you want me to help you, you'll have to ask politely instead of shouting orders all the time.*

**60.11** **throw** one's **weight about/around**
be bossy, enjoy giving orders to people
*Mick's always throwing his weight about and telling people what to do.*

**60.12** **red tape**
official rules, regulations and formal details
*There's too much red tape in our organisation. Everyone's tired of all the silly rules which make it difficult to do things quickly.*

**60.13** **with a heavy hand**
(too) firmly, with (too) much control
*The president seemed to rule the country with a heavy hand: everyone was afraid of him.*

**60.14** **make one's presence felt/make oneself felt**
make people aware of one's importance (through one's behaviour)
*The inspector certainly made his presence felt at the factory. He asked a lot of questions and checked everything carefully.*

**60.15** **send** someone **packing**
send someone away (angrily or because one dislikes him/her)
*When Charlie began to argue and shout, Mr Wright took him to the door and sent him packing.*

60.16 **have/hold** someone **in the palm of** one's **hand**
have someone completely in one's power or under one's influence
*Anna **has** James **in the palm of her hand**: he'll do anything for her.*

60.17 **have/keep** someone **on a string**
have/keep someone under one's control
*Don't **keep** Mike **on a string** by continually promising to increase his salary.*

60.18 **wear the trousers/pants**
be the dominant partner, be the master (usually in a marriage)
*Mrs Harris **wears the trousers** at home: Mr Harris is far too quiet and easy-going to argue with her.*

60.19 **do's and don'ts**
rules, regulations
*There are too many **do's and don'ts** in this job. I feel I have no freedom at all to make any decisions.*

60.20 **under** someone's **heel**
under someone's control
*Paul really is **under the heel** of his wife and has to do everything he is told.*

60.21 **at** someone's **beck and call**
always ready to obey someone, constantly willing to carry out a person's wishes
*Old Mrs Jameson likes to have everyone **at her beck and call**. She has her two daughters running backwards and forwards, doing things for her.*

60.22 **toe the line**
obey orders, behave as one is expected
*The new manager told his staff to **toe the line** and obey his instructions exactly.*

60.23 **at** someone's **feet**
ready to serve someone, under someone's influence, at someone's disposal
*Harry is young and successful: the whole world seems to be **at his feet**.*

60.24 **go by the book**
do something strictly according to the rules
*Jonathan always **goes by the book**: I doubt if he will let you do what you want.*

60.25 **(keep to) the letter of the law**
(follow) the exact meaning of the words of a rule or law (and obey it)
*Actually, John didn't **keep to the letter of the law** when he found the thief in his flat and hit him with the bottle.*

60.26 **take the law into** one's **own hands**
do oneself what one thinks is right instead of relying on the law, the police, etc.
*You cannot **take the law into your own hands** and shoot a burglar: you must call the police.*

60.27 **know which side** one's **bread is buttered on**
know what to do to please someone in authority
*I'm sure Henry will agree with his boss: he **knows which side his bread is buttered on**.*

60.28 **the tail wagging the dog**
the wrong person or thing being in control (often the exact opposite of what one would expect)

*Mr Small is not strong enough to control his employees. They do what they like —
it is a case of **the tail wagging the dog**.*

60.29   **leave** someone **to his/her own devices**

leave someone to do whatever they want

*Left to their **own devices**, the children made a mess of the room.*

60.30   **have no business** to do/doing something

have no right or authority to do something

*You **have no business** telling me what to do. You aren't my boss.*

60.31   **be none of** someone's **business**

be no concern of someone else

*You have every right to ask what I do every day at the office, but **it's none of your
business** what I do at home.*

60.32   **Mind your own business** [!]

Don't interfere. It's no concern of yours. (impolite)

*When we asked Mr Wilson why he was shouting at his son, he told us to **mind our
own business**.*

60.33   **get out of hand**

become out of control

*An angry crowd gathered and things soon **got out of hand**. Even the police found
it hard to control the situation.*

## 61. RESPONSIBILITY

61.1   **at the back of**

responsible for something (usually bad)

*I suppose Mr Tillotson is **at the back of** the plan to demolish those fine old
buildings.*

61.2   **on** one's **hands**

coming as an unwelcome responsibility

*I have far too much to do already without having this extra work **on my hands**.*

61.3   **hold the fort**

take charge of something (e.g. a business, an activity) during
someone's absence

*I am alone in the shop. Please come in and **hold the fort** while I go to see the
doctor.*

61.4   **leave** someone **holding the baby**

let someone else take care of something, e.g. a problem (often used in
the passive: **be left holding the baby**)

*John and I were partners in the business. But he went on a long holiday for health
reasons, and I **was left holding the baby**.*

61.5   **on** one's **own head**

one's own fault (for any harm that may occur)

*Alex never wears a seat belt: it'll be **on his own head** if he's ever injured in an
accident.*

61.6   **a millstone round** someone's **neck**

a heavy burden or responsibility (often causing trouble or making
progress difficult)

*This house is **a millstone round my neck**. It costs so much money to maintain and
repair that I can't afford to keep it any longer.*

**61.7    a cross (one has) to bear**

a responsibility or burden which causes suffering but which one cannot give up

*Tina's husband is an invalid now, and she has to look after him. It's **a cross she'll have to bear** for the rest of her life.*

**61.8    in the firing line**

in a position (of responsibility) which may be attacked

*You're the person who will have to explain the new production methods to the employees: so I'm afraid you'll be **in the firing line**.*

**61.9    carry the can**

take responsibility for something which has gone wrong (especially something done by others)

*Why do I always have to **carry the can** for other people's mistakes?*

**61.10    have enough/a lot/etc. on one's plate**

responsible for a lot of things

*Helen **has** quite **enough on her plate** without having to do this extra work.*

**61.11    pull one's weight**

do one's share of work, accept one's share of responsibility

*Peter doesn't **pull his weight** — he leaves too much of the work for me to do.*

**61.12    pass the buck**

pass on to someone else one's own responsibility for something

*Mr Small always **passes the buck** when something goes wrong. I've rarely seen him take the blame himself.*

**61.13    have someone's blood on one's hands**

be responsible for someone's death

*I was to blame for the accident in which Bob died and I feel I **have his blood on my hands**.*

**61.14    step into someone's shoes**

take over someone's duties, responsibilities, job, etc.

*When the supervisor retires next year, I shall **step into his shoes** and take over almost all his duties.*

**61.15    be no skin off someone's nose** ⚠

not be someone's concern or responsibility (because it does not affect them)

*I don't care whether he loses his job or not. **It's no skin off my nose**.*

**61.16    wash one's hands of someone/something**

refuse to take any further responsibility for someone/something

*Richard is not a reliable person. Appoint him if you wish — I **wash my hands of** the whole matter.*

**61.17    make a man of someone**

develop (a boy, etc.) into a responsible and independent adult

*Joining the local football team has **made a man of** Eric. The influence of the other members has done him a lot of good.*

## 62. PREVENTING

**62.1    put one's foot down**

not allow (someone to do) something

*You're always asking for time off but I'm going to **put my foot down** and refuse.*

62.2 **stand in** someone's/something's **way**
prevent someone from doing something/prevent something from happening
*If you wish to apply for the job, I'll not **stand in your way**. I hope you get it.*

62.3 **pour/throw cold water over/on**
try to prevent by discouraging and pointing out all the problems
*Bridget **poured cold water on** the idea of crossing the mountains in winter, pointing out all the difficulties.*

62.4 **keep/hold** someone/something **at bay**
prevent someone/something harmful from coming too close
*Although the wolves tried to attack us, we managed to **keep them at bay** by shooting several of them.*

62.5 **bound/tied hand and foot**
prevented from doing something (usually by rules)
*I wanted to change the way the club operated, but I was **bound hand and foot** by rules which had existed for a hundred years.*

62.6 **over my dead body**
not if I can possibly prevent it
*"Can I borrow your car, Dad?"*
*"**Over my dead body** — it's much too powerful for you to drive."*

# 63. PERSUASION, INFLUENCE

63.1 **twist** someone's **arm**
persuade someone (who may be unwilling) to do something
*If Sarah **twists** her mother's **arm**, I'm sure she'll be allowed to buy the new coat she wants.*

63.2 **lead** someone **by the nose**
have influence over someone so that one gets whatever one wants
*John's girlfriend **leads him by the nose**: he'll do anything she wishes.*

63.3 **make a/one's pitch/play** for
set out to get something by means of persuasion or influence
*Mary **made a play** for Jonathan as soon as she met him. "I'm going to marry that boy," she told her friend.*

63.4 **take** something **to heart**
be greatly influenced by something (especially advice)
*He must have **taken** my remarks **to heart** because he has done everything I suggested.*

63.5 **pull (a few) strings/wires**
obtain something through the influence of people one knows
*Do you know anyone who can **pull a few strings** and help us to get a passport in time for our holidays?*

63.6 **turn** someone's **head**
influence someone so that he/she becomes foolishly proud
*Marrying a rich man has **turned** Gay's **head** — she won't even talk to her old friends now.*

63.7   **tip the balance**
       **turn/tip the scales**
       influence the outcome of an event when several outcomes are possible
       (i.e. when the outcome is uncertain)
       *It was the chief engineer's influence which **tipped the scales** in favour of those who*
       *wanted to buy the new machine.*

63.8   **leave/make** one's/its **mark**
       make a firm or permanent impression
       *The jail sentence Joe Higgs served **left its mark** on him and he is now much quieter*
       *than before.*

63.9   **speak for itself/themselves**
       have qualities which are immediately obvious, without any further
       persuasion being needed
       *Miss Green's record **speaks for itself**: her previous successes are well-known to*
       *everyone.*

63.10  **(like)putty in** someone's **hands**
       easily influenced by someone
       *Charles is **like putty in** his wife's **hands**. She's only got to say what she wants and*
       *he gives it to her.*

63.11  **on the strength of** something
       encouraged by something, relying on something
       *Mr Small bought his new car **on the strength of** what his friend told him about it.*

63.12  **take** one's **cue from** someone/something
       use someone/something as a guide or model
       *Margaret **took her cue from** her friends, who always shopped at the supermarket.*
       *She now does the same herself.*

63.13  **sweet talk**
       talk in order to influence someone (often using pleasant or
       complimentary phrases)
       *That's **sweet talk**, Jill. I know you're trying to persuade me to cook a meal for*
       *you.*
       *Don't let Ann **sweet talk** you into getting what she wants.*
       *(Note: **sweet talk** can be used as a verb or noun)*

63.14  **talk** someone **into** doing something.
       Opposite: **talk** someone **out of** doing something
       persuade someone to do something
       *Who **talked** you **into** going on such a dangerous journey?*

63.15  **(have) the gift of the gab**
       (have) the ability to persuade people by talking well, talk easily and
       effectively
       *Monty **has the gift of the gab**. People enjoy listening to him, and he usually gets*
       *what he wants.*

63.16  **put words into** someone's **mouth**
       suggest to someone what his answer should be to a particular question.
       *The lawyer was told by the judge not to **put words into** his client's **mouth** in an*
       *effort to obtain the answers he wanted.*

**63.17 give a dog a bad name (and hang him)**
once bad things are said about a person, people will believe anything bad of him
*After Peter said Bob was a liar, people began to believe that Bob was bad in every way. It was a case of **give a dog a bad name and hang him**.*

**63.18 under** someone's **thumb**
completely under the influence or control of someone
*Bill Peel is **under** his mother's **thumb**. I'm sure he'll never get married because she won't let him.*

**63.19 wheels within wheels**
different influences (often working secretly)
*I'm sure Mr Hind will get the job. He knows one of the manager's assistants, and there are **wheels within wheels**.*

**63.20 stack the cards/odds against** someone
reduce someone's chances of winning, make it difficult for someone to succeed
*I doubt if you'll get the job. You didn't go to a good school, and so **the cards are stacked against** you.*

**63.21 cut no ice with** someone
fail to influence or impress someone, have no effect on someone
*Your arguments **cut no ice with** me. I'm not impressed at all by what you say.*

**63.22 sit tight**
wait and not allow oneself to be influenced by others
*I don't like the suggestion that you should lower the price of your car. I think you should **sit tight** and try to get the price you've asked for.*

**63.23 stand/turn** something **on its head**
reverse completely an idea or an argument
*He is now saying exactly the opposite of what he said last week. He has **turned** the whole idea **on its head**.*

**63.24 if** someone's **got anything to do with it**
if someone has any influence or power in the situation
*"Do you think Bill Jones will get the job?"*
*"No. At least, not **if I've got anything to do with it**."*

**63.25 go over** someone's **head**
go beyond a person in a lower position to someone more important
*If you won't listen to my proposal, I shall have to **go over your head** and put it to your boss.*

# 64. SHARING, PARTICIPATING

**64.1 throw in** one's **lot** with someone
join with someone and share his good or bad fortune
*I'm going to leave my firm and **throw in my lot** with our chief competitors. They have offered me a much better job.*

**64.2 go halves**
share the cost of something
*Richard and Mary are both working and **go halves** with the cost of everything they buy.*

64.3 **go Dutch**
share the cost of an expense, especially a meal
*When we go out together for a meal, my girlfriend and I always **go Dutch** — each of us pays half.*

64.4 **get in on the act** 🔲
do something which others are doing so that one can share in their success
*Everyone is busy making and selling things to tourists in this town. Why don't we **get in on the act**? We could make a lot of money out of it.*

64.5 **hand in glove** (with someone)
in close co-operation with, usually for some bad purpose
*Some of the employees are **hand in glove** with the security men at the gate and can walk out with things belonging to the company.*

64.6 **common ground**
ideas, beliefs, etc. which are shared
*I see we're on **common ground**: we both have the same ideas about politics.*

64.7 **shoulder to shoulder**
on the same side, in complete agreement
*Let's go forward **shoulder to shoulder**. Then we're bound to win.*

## 65. THREATENING, WARNING

65.1 **hold** someone/a country/etc. **to ransom**
demand something by means of threats
*Mr Johnson's customers **held him to ransom** by saying they would not do business with him unless he reduced his prices.*

65.2 **put the screws on** someone
use threats or pressure to make someone do something
*It's time to **put the screws on** that company. Let's tell them we'll take them to court unless they pay the money they owe us.*

65.3 **hold a pistol/gun to** someone's **head**
force someone to do something by threatening him
*The manager **held a pistol to my head** and told me I would be dismissed if I did not do this extra work.*

65.4 **for two pins**
given the smallest additional reason (often used to introduce a threat)
***For two pins**, I'd leave and go home now. No one is talking sensibly.*

65.5 **Two can play at that game.**
The victim of a harmful action can do the same thing to the person who did the action.
*My neighbour played his stereo set very loudly to annoy me. But **two can play at that game**. Tonight I'll turn my TV up to keep him awake.*

65.6 **watch** one's **step**
be careful not to do anything wrong
*You'd better **watch your step** and not make that mistake again.*

65.7 **Watch it!** 🔲
Be careful!
***Watch it!** I'll knock you down if you make any more insulting remarks like that.*

65.8 **Steady on!**
Be careful! Slow down!
*Steady on! You're driving too fast on this narrow road.*

65.9 **Cut it out** ⚠️
Stop doing (something bad).
*Cut it out! I'm tired of your bad behaviour.*

65.10 **Jump to it!**
Hurry up! Obey immediately!
*Jump to it! The taxi has arrived to take us to the station.*

## 66. PUNISHMENT

66.1 **send** someone **to Coventry**
punish a person by refusing to speak to him/her
*Harold was sent to Coventry for not joining the strike. None of his workmates spoke to him for over a month.*

66.2 **be for the high jump** ⚠️
be about to be punished severely
*Ted will be for the high jump if he doesn't improve his work. His teacher will send him to see the headmaster.*

66.3 **throw the book at** someone
punish someone severely, bring all possible charges against someone
*The officer said that if any soldiers disobeyed his orders, he would throw the book at them.*

66.4 **get/receive** one's **just deserts**
be treated in the (bad) way which one deserves, be punished for something wrong
*Jimmy always finished with his girlfriends after only a few weeks. Now Linda has left him, and so he's got his just deserts.*

66.5 **serve** someone **right**
be a punishment which is deserved
*It serves Dave right to be kept in after school. He shouldn't have been fighting in the playground.*

66.6 **one in the eye for** someone
a punishment or experience which someone deserves
*It was one in the eye for him when he lost the match after boasting how good he was.*

66.7 **face the music**
face the unpleasant experience (e.g. punishment, reprimand) for something one has done
*When I go back to the office, I shall have to face the music for taking the day off without permission.*

66.8 **get** one's **marching orders**
be dismissed from one's job or position, be sent away
*Miss Wallace got her marching orders because her work was unsatisfactory. She was told not to come back.*

**66.9   get the sack**

be dismissed from one's job

*I **got the sack** at work today. They dismissed me because they said I was never punctual.*

**66.10   for one's sins**

as a punishment (used humorously)

***For my sins**, I've just been told I'll have to sing two songs at the concert instead of one.*

**66.11   six of the best**

physical punishment (i.e. six strokes with a cane)

*The headmaster gave Alan **six of the best** for not behaving himself in class.*

**66.12   a/the whipping boy**

someone who is punished instead of the person who has done something wrong

*I am **the whipping boy** for all the staff. I have to take the blame for everything that goes wrong.*

**66.13   put someone behind bars**

send someone to prison

*It's time a lot of football hooligans were **put behind bars**.*

**66.14   do/serve time**

be in prison

*John **served time** a few years ago. In fact, he was in prison for three years.*

**66.15   get away with (blue) murder**

do any bad thing one wants without being punished in any way

*She can do no wrong in the manager's opinion, and so she thinks she can **get away with murder**.*

**66.16   go/get off scot-free**

be completely free or unpunished (often after appearing in court)

*The court dismissed all the charges the police brought against him, and he **got off scot-free**.*

**66.17   be cruel to be kind**

treat someone harshly, or punish him, in order to benefit him (sometimes used humorously)

*Sometimes you must **be cruel to be kind**, and so the teacher made Harry stay in after class to teach him a lesson!*


## 67. REVENGE

**67.1   get one's own back**

take revenge

*I'll **get my own back** on you for reporting me to the police.*

**67.2   have an account/a score to settle with someone**

have reason to take revenge on someone

*I've **an account to settle with** him and so I'm going to tell the police what he did last week.*

**67.3   pay someone back (with interest)**

take revenge on someone (causing even more harm than that person did to one originally)

*John insulted Sarah in public, but she **paid him back with interest**. She said very bad things about him in front of his employer.*

67.4    **a dose/taste of** one's **own medicine**
the same (unpleasant) treatment as one has already given or received
*Henry often makes unpleasant remarks to people. We should give him **a taste of his own medicine** and speak to him in the same way.*

# 68. VIOLENCE, CRUELTY

68.1    **raise/lift** one's/a **hand against** someone
threaten to hit or hurt someone
*I wouldn't **lift a hand against** Ted. He's always been helpful to me.*

68.2    **knock** someone's **block off** !
hit someone on the head (chiefly used as a threat)
*"I'll **knock** your **block off** if you do that again," Ken told the man who had just insulted him.*

68.3    **beat/knock, etc. the (living) daylights out of** someone
beat someone violently (often used in threats)
*Stop annoying my sister. If I see you near her again, I'll **knock the living daylights out of** you.*

68.4    **send/knock** someone/something **flying**
hit someone/something so that he/she/it falls over
*The car hit the old woman and **knocked her flying**.*

68.5    **give** someone **a thick ear**
hit someone over the ear (often used figuratively in threats)
*My wife will **give me a thick ear** when I get home for being so late!*

68.6    **go/be at it hammer and tongs**
fight or quarrel violently with someone
*Mr and Mrs Hickson went **at it hammer and tongs** when they got home. They woke all their neighbours with their quarrelling.*

68.7    **put the boot in**
attack someone unfairly and cruelly (someone whom one has already treated badly)
*After giving Mr Wright a difficult and unpleasant job to do, the company **put the boot in** and reduced his salary.*

68.8    **ride roughshod over** someone/something
treat someone/something in a cruel, unsympathetic way
*The manageress **rode roughshod over** all her staff, and several left because they couldn't stand such treatment.*

68.9    **the law of the jungle**
principles for surviving in a violent and dangerous situation, no rules at all
*This is a dangerous and violent city. In some parts of it, the only law is **the law of the jungle**.*

68.10   **(not) have the heart to** do something
(not) be unkind or cruel enough (to do something unpleasant)
*I **haven't the heart to** tell her that her cat has been run over. I wish I didn't have to do it.*

## 69. PERMISSION

69.1   **have/be given a free hand**
         (have/be given) freedom to do whatever one wants
         *I've **been given a free hand** to reorganise the office as I want.*

69.2   **get/be given the green light**
         (get/be given) permission to go ahead (with something)
         *The new project has **been given the green light** and work on building the road will begin next month.*

69.3   **take the liberty of** doing something
         do something without obtaining permission
         *The housekeeper told me she had **taken the liberty of** tidying up my room although she knew I did not really want her to do so.*

69.4   **lend** one's **name to** something
         give permission for one's name to be used to support something
         *The film star **lent his name to** the efforts to raise money to help the flood victims.*

69.5   **overstep/overshoot the mark**
         do more than is allowed
         *Lorna **overstepped the mark** when she told her assistant to take the day off. She had no authority to do so.*

69.6   **take French leave**
         leave or be absent without permission (old-fashioned but still used occasionally)
         *I wanted to go to the football match, and so I **took French leave** from the office. Unfortunately, the boss found out and told me to get his permission in future.*

## 70. DEPENDENCE

70.1   **tied to** someone's (a mother's or wife's) **apron strings**
         completely ruled by or dependent upon one's mother or wife
         *John is **tied to** his mother's **apron strings**. She decides everything in his life.*

70.2   **under** someone's **wing**
         in the care of someone
         *Jane has taken that new child **under her wing** and is looking after him very well.*

70.3   **set/lay great store by** something
         Opposite: **set/lay little store by** something
         attach high value to something, depend a lot on something (often for forming one's opinions)
         *Sylvia **sets great store by** her husband's judgement and never questions his decisions.*

## 71. INDEPENDENCE

71.1   **go** one's **own way**
         act independently (usually against others' advice)
         *I'm **going my own way** in this matter and will not be influenced by others.*

71.2   do something **off** one's **own bat**
         do something completely by oneself without being told to by anyone
         *Mary is decorating the shop **off her own bat**. Nobody has ever told her to do so.*

71.3 **have a mind of** one's **own**
  be independent, be able to think independently
  *I doubt if you'll persuade Robin to do it: **he has a mind of his own**.*

71.4 **paddle** one's **own canoe**
  be independent, do something on one's own, control one's own affairs
  *Harry didn't want his father to help him get a job. "I'll **paddle my own canoe**," he said.*

71.5 **in** one's **own right**
  independently, not because of someone else
  *The film-star's daughter became a famous actress **in her own right**. No one could say that her success was due to her father's fame.*

## 72. HELPING, ASSISTING

72.1 **give/lend a (helping) hand**
  help
  *I'll always **give** Jenny **a helping hand** any time she needs a job done in her house.*

72.2 **do** someone **a good turn**
  Opposite: **do** someone **a bad turn**
  do something helpful for someone
  *John **did me a good turn**, and so I'll help him whenever I can.*

72.3 **do well by** someone
  treat someone generously, help someone by giving money
  *The firm has always **done** very **well by** Mr Potterton, giving him an increase in salary every year.*

72.4 **You scratch my back and I'll scratch yours.** [!]
  If you help me, I'll help you.
  *If you write a good report about me, I'll help you to get some new furniture for your office. **You scratch my back and I'll scratch yours**.*

72.5 **put in/say a good word for** someone
  praise someone in order to help him/her
  *I'll **put in a good word for** Elsie when I see the manager. I'd like her to get the job.*

72.6 **save** one's **(own) skin/neck/bacon** [!]
  help oneself/someone to escape from danger, save one's/someone's life
  *The villager lied to the police to **save his own skin**.*

72.7 **do the honours**
  act as host, help guests by serving them
  *The coffee is in the kitchen, Jim. Will you **do the honours** and serve it?*

72.8 **a tower of strength**
  someone who can be depended on to give help or comfort (usually in difficult times)
  *Sheila is **a tower of strength** to the elderly people next door and is always ready to help them.*

72.9 **driving force**
  someone (energetic) who encourages a plan, an activity, etc.
  *The assistant manager is the real **driving force** in the company.*

72.10 someone's **right hand man**
  someone's chief helper
  *Bill is the manager's **right hand man** and can take charge when he is away.*

72.11 **a good Samaritan**
someone who helps others in trouble or in need
*Ted really is **a good Samaritan** and will always help people in need.*

72.12 **a shot in the arm**
help and encouragement to someone/something (e.g. a business) when it is badly needed
*When the young writer won a prize in the story competition, it was **a shot in the arm** for him. He had started to lose all hope of success.*

72.13 **a step in the right direction**
Opposite: **a step in the the wrong direction**
an action which helps to improve a situation
*The changes in the education system are **a step in the right direction** and will improve the teaching in our schools.*

72.14 **the old boy network**
a system in which people help the people they know to get jobs, etc.
*"Go and see Mr Smith if you want a job, and mention my name. We were at the same school and he'll help if he can." "I see. It's **the old boy network**."*

72.15 **under** one's **own steam**
all by one's own efforts, without help from others
*I'm going to the party **under my own steam** as I don't wish to depend on others for transport.*

72.16 **with no strings attached**
(given) without any special conditions
*The government lent the money to the company **with no strings attached**.*

72.17 **pull the carpet/rug from under** someone
stop giving someone help without any warning
*When Jane's uncle stopped giving her a loan half-way through her university education, it **pulled the carpet from under** her.*

72.18 someone's **best bet**
the best thing someone can do in a situation, someone's best hope (usually used to advise people)
*It will probably rain tomorrow. Your **best bet** is to hold a party for the children indoors.*

## 73. KINDNESS, SYMPATHY

73.1 One's **heart goes out to** someone
One feels pity or sympathy for someone. (used to show sympathy)
*My **heart goes out to** Mrs Jones. The man who broke into her house took all her money.*

73.2 **My heart bleeds for you**
I feel very sorry for you. (often used humorously)
*"Oh dear, I'm getting so poor that I've got to sell one of my three cars." "Really, **my heart bleeds for you**."*

73.3 **Have a heart** [!]
Be kind, be reasonable [!]
***Have a heart!** I can't possibly get through that amount of work in such a short time.*

73.4 **have** one's **heart in the right place/have a heart of gold**
be a kind and sympathetic person
*Jane will help her friends in any way she can. She **has a heart of gold/Her heart is in the right place.***

73.5 **open-handed**
generous
*Other countries were not so **open-handed** and refused to pay the expenses of their delegates.*

73.6 **go easy on** someone
not treat someone too harshly
***Go easy on** Ben: he's only very young and he tries hard.*

73.7 **Hard lines!**
used to show sympathy and understanding
***Hard lines!** You only just missed the centre of the target with that shot.*

73.8 **Hard cheese!** ⚠
used to show sympathy and understanding, but slightly humorous
***Hard cheese!** The horse you bet on should have won the race instead of coming second.*

73.9 **turn the other cheek**
forgive, not take revenge
*Instead of losing his temper when he was insulted, Robert merely **turned the other cheek**.*

73.10 **a shoulder to cry on**
someone who will sympathise with one in times of trouble
*She doesn't want to be told what to do. She needs sympathy — **a shoulder to cry on**.*

73.11 **give** someone **short shrift**
be unsympathetic or unfriendly to someone
*Ann came to me with a lot of complaints about the company, but I **gave her short shrift** and told her not to be silly.*

## 74. WORRY, ANXIETY

74.1 **hold** one's **breath**
wait anxiously (i.e. stop breathing because one is very anxious)
*Katie **held her breath** as the aircraft landed, hoping everything would be all right.*

74.2 **have** something **hanging over** one's **head**
be in constant danger of something which may happen
*The possibility that he would fail in the examinations **hung over his head** all year.*

74.3 **(be/get) in a stew**
(be/become) very anxious
*Florence **gets in a stew** about little things that don't matter very much and she always looks anxious.*

74.4 **have butterflies in** one's **stomach**
feel very nervous
*I **had butterflies in my stomach** when I went to see the dentist.*

74.5 **have** something **on** one's **mind**
think about something which worries one
*Chris looks as though he **has something on his mind**. Perhaps he's worried about the meeting tomorrow.*

74.6    **get/have** one's **knickers in a twist** !

become/be very confused or worried (often used humorously but it
may give offence)

*Betty's **got her knickers in a twist** over the speech she will have to make at the
wedding. She feels certain she can't do it.*

74.7    **tear** one's **hair out**

be very worried or irritated (about something)

*The boss is in a terrible mood this morning. He's **tearing his hair out** because the
job won't be finished in time.*

74.8    **get/have cold feet**

become/be nervous or frightened, especially when faced with a difficult
situation

*Jenny **has cold feet** now that the time has come to move into her new house. She
isn't at all sure she wants to go.*

74.9    **like a cat on hot bricks**

very nervous

*What's the matter with Betty Hanson? She isn't at all relaxed: she's **like a cat on
hot bricks**.*

74.10   **worry** someone **to death**

make someone extremely worried

*It **worries me to death** to see you looking so tired.*

74.11   **not cross** one's **bridges before** one **comes to them**

not worry unnecessarily about future problems until they happen

*Don't worry about what might happen if the weather causes the match to be
postponed. Let's **not cross our bridges before we come to them**.*

74.12   **all of a flutter**

excited, worried

*Mrs Rumbold is **all of a flutter** about her daughter's wedding next week.*

74.13   **on tenterhooks**

feeling anxious and apprehensive (while waiting for something)

*I'm **on tenterhooks** about the examination results — I do want to do well.*

74.14   **ill at ease**

nervous, uncomfortable

*John was **ill at ease** during his interview, which was far more difficult than he
expected.*

74.15   **mind/watch** one's **P's and Q's**

take care to behave well

*Watch your **P's and Q's** or else you won't be invited to their house again.*

74.16   **get** something **out of** one's **system**

express one's feelings or do something to stop worrying

*I had to tell them how angry I was to **get** the matter **out of my system**.*

74.17   **clear the air**

reduce tension (through speaking plainly or saying what one really
thinks)

*At last, we said what we really thought of each other. I know we were both very
angry but it **cleared the air**.*

74.18   **(be able to) breathe again**

be relieved or less worried (after a difficult time)

*I'm **able to breathe again** now that my wife has recovered from her illness.*

74.19 **devil-may-care**

completely unworried about what one does

*Peter has a **devil-may-care** attitude to life. He'll quite happily go anywhere or do anything.*

74.20 **not lose any/much sleep over** something

not worry about something

*The mistake you made isn't at all important. Please **don't lose any sleep over** it.*

74.21 **not care/give two hoots** about something ⚠

not care at all about something

*I couldn't **give two hoots** whether he was bored or not. I think it was a very interesting talk.*

74.22 **take it easy**

not hurry, not become anxious, not do too much

*The doctor told James to **take it easy** and not to work too hard.*


## 75. REASSURANCE

75.1 **put/set** someone's **mind at rest**

reassure someone, help him/her to stop worrying

*Mr Hickson **put** Claire's **mind at rest** and told her that she'd got the job.*

75.2 **put (new/fresh) heart into** someone

encourage someone, make him/her more hopeful

*The goal he scored, **put fresh heart into** the team and they were soon playing well again.*

75.3 **take heart**

Opposite: **lose heart**

be encouraged, become more confident

***Take heart!** We haven't far to climb to get to the top.*

75.4 **never mind.**

Don't worry. (used to reassure people)

*"I'm sorry. I've broken one of your cups."*

*"Oh, **never mind**. We have plenty more."*

75.5 **It's not the end of the world.**

It's not as bad as you think.

*Even if George's left you, **it's not the end of the world**. I'm sure you'll meet someone else.*

75.6 **There'll always be a next time.**

There will always be another opportunity to succeed. (used to reassure and encourage)

*Never mind about losing the race. **There's always a next time** — you can try again next year.*


## 76. ANGER, ANNOYANCE, INDIGNATION

76.1 **get** someone's **blood up**

make someone angry

*He **got my blood up** by criticising my best friend. I lost my temper and almost hit him.*

**76.2    make** someone's **blood boil**
make someone extremely angry
*It **made my blood boil** to hear the insulting things he was saying about my brother.*

**76.3    burst a blood-vessel**
become very angry or excited
*There's no need to **burst a blood-vessel** just because the referee made the wrong decision.*

**76.4    go off (at) the deep end**
lose one's temper, become very angry
*When his secretary told him she had forgotten to book his hotel room, John **went off at the deep end** and began to shout at her.*

**76.5    fly off the handle**
lose one's temper
*Whenever Sandra's small children will not do as they are told, she **flies off the handle** and smacks them.*

**76.6    make** someone's **hackles rise**
make someone very angry
*It **made** Ted's **hackles rise** when Mr Smart criticised his report without even reading it carefully.*

**76.7    do** one's **nut** ⚠
become very angry
*Elizabeth had an accident in her father's car and damaged it slightly. "Oh dear, my dad will **do his nut** when he sees what I've done," she said to Ann.*

**76.8    go through the roof/hit the roof/ceiling**
become very angry, lose one's temper
*When James was late for work the fifth morning in succession, his boss **hit the roof** and threatened him with dismissal.*

**76.9    blow** one's **top**
become very angry, lose one's temper
*When the goalkeeper failed to catch the ball, the captain of the team **blew his top**.*

**76.10   get/be (all) steamed up**
become/be very upset or angry
*The trouble with Mr Reynolds is that he **gets all steamed up** whenever anyone makes a mistake.*

**76.11   hot under the collar**
very angry, very emotional
*There's no need to get **hot under the collar** at Susie's remarks — she didn't mean to offend you.*

**76.12   see red**
become angry
*It makes me **see red** when someone borrows my English book and forgets to return it.*

**76.13   let off steam**
get rid of (i.e. show) one's anger, emotions
*When Bill was told off for not wearing a tie, he **let off steam** by telling his boss what he thought of her.*

**76.14   make the sparks fly**
argue with someone, cause someone to argue or show anger
*Mrs Barber **made the sparks fly** at the staff meeting today by saying that some teachers were neglecting their responsibilities.*

76.15 **jump down** someone's **throat**

angrily disagree with someone, attack someone verbally

*When I gave my opinion at the meeting, Bill suddenly **jumped down my throat** and accused me of causing trouble.*

76.16 **give** someone a **piece of** one's **mind**

speak angrily and frankly to someone, scold someone

*Carol **gave Tom a piece of her mind** for coming into the house with dirty shoes.*

76.17 **rant and rave**

talk angrily, loudly and irrationally about something

*Tina and I were walking past someone's house last night when suddenly a man came out and started **ranting and raving**, accusing us of stealing his vegetables.*

76.18 **drive/send** someone **up the wall**

make someone very angry or confused

*All these silly arguments are **driving me up the wall**. I don't understand how people can say such things.*

76.19 **bite/snap** someone's **head off**

answer sharply and angrily (often shouting or scolding)

*There's no need to **bite my head off**. I only asked you a question — I wasn't criticising you.*

76.20 **let fly at** someone

shout angrily or speak sharply to someone, strike (someone)

*Mary **let fly at** her little boy when he kept on talking, but I really think she shouldn't have been so angry.*

76.21 **look daggers at** someone

look angrily at someone (generally without speaking)

*She didn't say anything when I told her to be quiet but she certainly **looked daggers at** me.*

76.22 **get off** someone's **back**

stop annoying or troubling someone

***Get off my back!** I am getting tired of you and your constant criticism!*

76.23 **get** someone's **goat**

annoy or irritate someone

*Henry **gets my goat** by always wanting a meal as soon as he comes home.*

76.24 **get in/into** someone's **hair**

be a cause of anger, irritation or anxiety to someone

*Peter is **getting in** Sylvia's **hair**. She's told him she doesn't want to see him, but he keeps on phoning her every day.*

76.25 **get on** someone's **nerves**

make someone annoyed or bad-tempered (by some continuous action)

*Stop drumming your fingers on the table — you're **getting on my nerves!***

76.26 **rub** someone **up the wrong way**

make someone feel hostile, antagonise someone

*Unfortunately, Arthur Stoke will never make a good salesman. He **rubs** people **up the wrong way** with his aggressive attitude.*

76.27 **get under** someone's **skin**

be a cause of continual (perhaps unreasonable) irritation or anxiety in someone

*I'm afraid that William Bold **gets under my skin**. He's always boasting about something.*

76.28  **be a pain in the neck** [!]
annoy someone, be a cause of irritation, tiredness or unhappiness
*John Lee's **a pain in the neck** at times: he never stops talking about himself.*

76.29  **tread/step on** someone's **toes**
upset someone, make someone annoyed (usually unintentionally)
*Be careful you don't **tread on** anyone's **toes** by being too critical at the meeting.*

76.30  **come to a pretty/fine pass**
reach such a bad state that it annoys one
*Things have **come to a pretty pass** when the food in the hotel is as bad as this. I can't possibly eat it.*

76.31  **It's too much/It's a bit much**
It's too much to be tolerated (used to show annoyance or indignation)
*It's **a bit much** when Helen's husband goes out every night and never takes her with him.*

76.32  **fall foul of** someone
do something that annoys someone
*I fell **foul of** my boss this morning by refusing to work late tonight.*

76.33  **ask for it/ask for trouble**
do something which may make others angry, behave so as to cause trouble
*You're **asking for trouble** if you continue to drive so fast. You're exceeding the speed limit.*

76.34  **enough to drive** someone **to drink**
very annoying (continuously, or over a long period)
*Stop annoying me with your criticisms. It's enough to **drive me to drink**!*

76.35  **make** someone **turn over in** his/her **grave**
be so bad that it would annoy a particular person if he or she were still alive
*Your father wouldn't have liked you to do this. It's enough to **make him turn over in his grave!***

76.36  **bad blood**
ill feeling, indignation
*There has been **bad blood** between the two of them ever since they had a family argument several years ago.*

76.37  **a chip on** one's **shoulder**
a feeling of anger, a sense of injustice (perhaps unreasonable)
*Tom **has a chip on his shoulder**. He thinks people are against him because of his family background, although he has no reason to think so.*

76.38  **kick oneself**
be angry with oneself for having done something wrong or having missed an opportunity
*I could **kick myself** for not having posted my application yesterday. Now it's too late.*

76.39  **on the warpath**
in an angry mood, ready to quarrel or attack someone (verbally)
*Be careful if you see the manager this morning. He's **on the warpath** about a complaint he received from a customer.*

76.40 **at each other's throats**

fighting or quarrelling angrily

*Sonia and her sister don't agree at all: they are always **at each other's throats**.*

76.41 **like a red rag to a bull**

certain to make someone angry

*Any criticism of Mr Stewart's daughter is **like a red rag to a bull**. He thinks she is absolutely perfect.*

76.42 **Of all the cheek!/Of all the nerve!**

used to show surprise and annoyance on hearing of someone's behaviour

*Well, **of all the cheek!** You might have asked me before you borrowed my book.*

76.43 **Get lost!** ☐!

**Go (and) jump in the river/lake/sea/ocean!** ☐!

**Take a running jump!** ☐!

**Go to blazes/hell!** ☐!

**Drop dead!** ☐!

used to show anger at what someone has said

***Get lost!/Go and jump in the lake!/ Take a running jump!/Go to blazes!/Drop dead!*** *I'm not going to work every weekend for nothing at all.*

76.44 **That does it!**

That's the end of something (used to show anger and a refusal to accept any more of something)

***That does it!*** *I'm not going to listen to any more of your insults.*

76.45 **Don't give me that** ☐!

Don't expect me to believe that!

***Don't give me that!*** *You can't expect anyone to believe such a story!*

76.46 **(You can) put that in your pipe and smoke it!** ☐!

used to add force to what one has said, especially something said in anger

*You're a lazy, stupid trouble-maker. Everyone here thinks the same about you — so **you can put that in your pipe and smoke it!***

76.47 **Keep your hair/shirt on!**

Don't get angry or excited.

***Keep your hair on!*** *This is an unimportant matter — nothing to get excited about.*

## 77. EXCITEMENT

77.1 **thrilled to bits**

very excited, highly delighted

*I'm **thrilled to bits** at the thought of going to France for our holiday — I know I'll enjoy it very much.*

77.2 **beside** oneself

very excited, very emotional

*Mary's husband has just been discharged from hospital and she's **beside herself** with joy.*

77.3 **all hot and bothered**

very excited, very upset

*Dorothy was **all hot and bothered** about so many people arriving for lunch. She had not been expecting visitors.*

**77.4** **in a flat spin**
  excited and confused
  *I've been in a flat spin trying to get everything ready for our holiday.*

**77.5** **lose** one's **cool**
  Opposite: **keep one's cool**
  lose control, become very emotional or excited
  *Even if you hear a lot of criticism at the meeting, don't lose your cool. It's important to keep calm.*

**77.6** **in the heat of the moment**
  while influenced by the excitement or emotion of a particular occasion.
  *In the heat of the moment, Harry swore at the referee and was sent off the field.*

**77.7** **make a song and dance** (about something)
  make an unnecessary fuss (about something)
  *I don't know why you're making such a song and dance about the changes in the timetable. They are only minor ones.*

**77.8** **stir the blood**
  make one excited (and hopeful or joyful)
  *The sight of the mountains in the distance is enough to stir the blood — it is very impressive indeed.*

**77.9** **a nail-biting finish/event/etc.**
  a very exciting finish/event/etc.
  *Two minutes before the end of the match, the other team scored a goal to make the scores level. It was a nail-biting finish!*

**77.10** **for kicks**
  for excitement and pleasure
  *I broke the shop window for kicks. I was bored and needed some excitement.*

**77.11** **the bright lights**
  the excitement of city life
  *Fiona would much rather be among the bright lights than in the country. She loves London.*


# 78. CALMNESS

**78.1** **keep** one's **head**
  Opposite: **lose** one's **head**
  stay calm
  *Keep your head and don't look down. The rescue party are climbing up the cliff to save us.*

**78.2** **take** something **in** one's **stride**
  accept something calmly without getting excited
  *John took the news of his transfer abroad in his stride and did not let it affect his work in any way.*

**78.3** **take the heat out of** something
  remove the excitement or emotion from something (e.g. a quarrel)
  *The two brothers were quarrelling angrily, but their sister took the heat out of the situation by taking them both out for a meal.*

**78.4** **Hold your horses!**
  Keep calm. Don't act too hastily.

*Hold your horses! We don't have to rush to the shop now. It's open till late tonight.*

78.5 **Keep your hair/shirt on!**
Keep calm. Don't get so annoyed.
*Keep your shirt on! I only asked you if Tina was still your girl-friend. There's no need to lose your temper.*

## 79. DELIGHT, ENJOYMENT

79.1 **tickled pink/to death**
delighted, very pleased
*We were **tickled pink** when we heard we had won the first prize.*

79.2 **on top of the world**
very happy and physically well
*Dave feels **on top of the world** since he passed his driving-test.*

79.3 **have the time of** one's **life**
have a very enjoyable time
*Susan seems to be **having the time of her life** at the fair. I haven't seen her so happy for a long time.*

79.4 **have a whale of a time**
have a very enjoyable time
*It was a great party. Everyone **had a whale of a time**.*

79.5 **fun and games**
used to refer to any enjoyable activity or lively behaviour
*We had **fun and games** at the staff meeting today. There was wine and a huge cake to celebrate someone's birthday.*

79.6 **in stitches**
in fits of laughter
*Jim told a few jokes at the party last evening and had everyone **in stitches**.*

## 80. HAPPINESS, PLEASURE

80.1 **all right**
well, happy
*"Are you **all right**?" "Yes, thanks. I'm having a very good time."*

80.2 **let** one's **hair down**
relax and enjoy oneself
*At the office party, a few people who were usually serious and quiet really **let their hair down**. They laughed loudly and started telling jokes.*

80.3 **full of the joys of spring**
very happy, talking happily
*The last time I saw Deborah, she was **full of the joys of spring**.*

80.4 **over the moon**
extremely happy and excited
*Brenda is thrilled about winning the sports competition. "I'm **over the moon**," she said.*

80.5 **in good heart**
happy and cheerful
*John is **in good heart**: his new business is doing really well.*

80.6   **the life of Riley**
       a happy and trouble-free life, with every luxury one wishes
       *I'm going to live the **life of Riley** now that I've won all this money.*

80.7   **be music to** someone's **ears**
       be very good news, be very welcome words to someone
       *When he told us about his plans to help the team, it was **music to our ears**. It gave us so much hope for the future.*

80.8   **a sight for sore eyes**
       a very pleasant and welcome sight
       *We were stranded on the mountain all night and the arrival of the rescue party was **a sight for sore eyes**.*

80.9   **the jet set**
       wealthy people who travel about a lot (often by air) and who have a good time.
       ***The jet set** have made this hotel very popular. Most come from abroad and spend a lot of money here.*

80.10  **sow** one's **wild oats**
       have a good time while one is young
       *It's all very well **sowing your wild oats** and having lots of girlfriends but you must still do some studying.*

80.11  **paint the town red**
       have a good time, enjoy oneself in a carefree (and noisy) way
       *Let's go out tonight and **paint the town red**. We've got no more worries about exams.*

80.12  **bend over backwards**
       **fall over** oneself
       try in every possible way to please someone
       *Laura **bends over backwards/falls over herself** trying to please her friends but they just take it as a matter of course.*

## 81. SADNESS, UNHAPPINESS

81.1   **have/make/pull a long face**
       look unhappy
       *He **pulled a long face** when the results of the competition were announced and found he hadn't won.*

81.2   **with a heavy heart**
       feeling sad, unhappy
       *I left the meeting **with a heavy heart**: all the suggestions I had made were ignored.*

81.3   **down in the dumps/mouth**
       depressed, miserable
       *Mary is **down in the dumps** because her husband has to go abroad for six months.*

81.4   **feel low**
       feel depressed, be unhappy
       *I felt low when the post arrived and there was no letter from my wife.*

81.5   **with** one's **tail between** one's **legs**
       in a miserable and ashamed manner
       *Philip's examination results were so poor that he had to leave the university and go home **with his tail between his legs**.*

**81.6**   **go (all) to pieces**

break down, become distressed, lose one's courage

*The team went **all to pieces** after the other team had scored three goals.*

**81.7**   **eat** one's **heart out**

be very sad or distressed

*John has been **eating his heart out** since Mary said she didn't wish to see him again.*

**81.8**   one's **heart sinks**

one is disappointed, one becomes sad

*I thought we had nearly reached the top of the hill and my **heart sank** when I found we had another kilometre to go.*

**81.9**   **upset** someone's/the **applecart**

spoil someone's plans or something which has been organised

*The teachers had made all the plans for the school picnic. But then it rained very heavily, and everywhere was flooded. That really **upset the applecart**.*

**81.10**   **break** someone's **heart**

distress someone, make someone very unhappy

*Sheila is very proud of her new car and it would **break her heart** if it were damaged.*

**81.11**   **cast a cloud over**

spoil by being worrying, unpleasant, etc.

*The assistant manager was very popular, and his dismissal has **cast a cloud over** the whole department.*

**81.12**   **laugh on the other side of** one's **face**

become sad or disappointed after being happy or successful

*"Some of you are laughing now," the teacher said to the pupils. "But you'll **laugh on the other side of your face** when I talk to your parents."*

**81.13**   **no laughing matter**

something very serious which may hurt or sadden one

*It's **no laughing matter**. Our failure to obtain this contract means that the firm may have to close down.*

**81.14**   **more's the pity**

and that's something to be sorry about

*The interesting buildings in the old part of the city are being replaced by modern office blocks, **more's the pity**.*

**81.15**   **take the rough with the smooth**

accept unhappy or difficult times with happy or easy ones

*I now have to travel much further to work than I used to. However, you have to **take the rough with the smooth** when you change your job.*

**81.16**   **have** one's **ups and downs**

have times of happiness and times of difficulty

*Our sales staff **have their ups and downs** selling these cars. Sometimes they are successful and sometimes not.*

## 82. INTEREST

**82.1**   **be/get bitten by the bug**

become very keen on something, take a great interest in something

*Alice has **been bitten by the** computer **bug** and talks about nothing else all day.*

82.2  **make it** one's **business to** do something
      be interested enough to do something which others have considered
      unnecessary or troublesome
      *The new teacher has **made it her business to** meet the parents of every pupil in her*
      *class.*

82.3  **poke** one's **nose into** something
      (used in a derogatory way) be concerned with someone else's business
      without a good reason
      *He's always **poking his nose into** my private affairs and telling me what to do.*

82.4  **a nosey Parker** [!]
      someone who is too curious about other people's business
      *Sandra is **a real nosey Parker** and always wants to know what everybody else is*
      *doing.*

## 83. BOREDOM

83.1  **kill time**
      do something to pass the time (thus avoiding boredom)
      *Selina is **killing time** while waiting for her plane by doing a crossword puzzle.*

83.2  **in a rut/groove**
      leading a boring and monotonous life
      *My job makes me feel that I'm **in a rut**. I do the same thing all day long.*

83.3  **fed up**
      bored, unhappy, annoyed
      *I'm **fed up**. I've got nothing to do and no one to talk to!*

83.4  **at a loose end**
      bored, having nothing to do
      *Mary was **at a loose end** yesterday afternoon. Eventually, she telephoned Daphne*
      *and arranged to go to the cinema with her.*

83.5  **a wet blanket**
      a miserable, boring person
      *Roger was **a wet blanket** at the party. He sat in a corner and never spoke to*
      *anyone.*

## 84. DETERMINATION

84.1  **mean business**
      be serious and determined
      *I **mean business** and will carry this job through to the end*

84.2  **go all out**
      be very determined, make every effort (to do something)
      *The champion **went all out** to win the table-tennis competition. I have never seen*
      *him play so well before.*

84.3  **He'll/I'll/etc. stop at nothing**
      He'll/I'll/etc. do anything, even if dishonest (to achieve something)
      *Don't trust him: **he'll stop at nothing** to get what he wants.*

84.4  **go to great/any/etc. length(s)**
      do everything possible (even dishonestly if necessary) in order to get
      something

*Mr Todd will* **go to any lengths** *to become manager of the company. I'm sure that anyone who stands in his way will be harmed.*

84.5　**move heaven and earth** to do something

do everything one possibly can (to achieve something)

*The police are* **moving heaven and earth** *to find the person who shot Mr Lee.*

84.6　**dig** one's **heels in**

be determined in one's refusal to do something, not to allow something

*Mrs Tyson* **dug her heels in** *and refused to say anything to the police unless her lawyer was present.*

84.7　**make/take** a/one's **stand**

be prepared or determined to resist or fight for something

*We must all* **take a stand** *against nuclear arms or else we'll destroy the whole world.*

84.8　**stand/hold** one's **ground**

remain firm (against an attack)

*Stella* **held her ground** *against several attempts to remove her as secretary of the tennis club.*

84.9　**stick to** one's **guns**

keep one's point of view in an argument, refuse to change one's opinions

*Many speakers at the meeting criticized John's report, but he* **stuck to his guns**, *saying he would not change a word of what he had said.*

84.10　**never say die**

never give up

*Never say die. You can't say you have lost the election until all the votes have been counted.*

84.11　**get/come to grips with** something

deal with a problem seriously and in a determined way

*We have been ignoring this problem for far too long and it is time we* **came to grips with** *it.*

84.12　**fight** someone/something **tooth and nail**

oppose someone/something with a lot of determination

*I will* **fight** *you* **tooth and nail** *if you put that suggestion to the management. I don't like it at all.*

## 85. DISAPPOINTMENT

85.1　**give** something **up as a bad job**

stop doing something because it is a failure or impossible

*There was no chance of climbing the mountain because of the mist, and so we* **gave it up as a bad job** *and went home.*

85.2　**more in sorrow than in anger**

more disappointed than angry

*"Will he ever succeed?" asked his father,* **more in sorrow than in anger**, *when he learnt that his son had failed in his examinations for the second time.*

85.3　**a bitter pill (to swallow)**

something unpleasant or disappointing which one has to accept

*I had expected to be given the new job at the office, and it was* **a bitter pill to swallow** *when I heard that it had been offered to someone else.*

85.4    **out of the frying pan (and) into the fire**
from one bad situation to another one even worse
*Pete left his job because he disliked his boss. But he dislikes his boss in his new job even more, so he's jumped **out of the frying pan into the fire**.*

85.5    **cold comfort**
no comfort at all
*It was **cold comfort** to Robert to learn that several other students in his class had failed in their examinations.*

## 86. BRAVERY

86.1    **keep a stiff upper lip**
remain calm and unafraid in the face of difficulty or opposition
*In spite of all the criticism he received, he **kept a stiff upper lip** and said nothing.*

86.2    **not turn a hair**
show no emotion at all when faced with some surprising occurrence or danger
*Alan did **not turn a hair** when he saw the bear coming towards him.*

86.3    **keep** one's **chin up**
remain cheerful, not become frightened or sad
***Keep your chin up** and try not to be disappointed at your lack of success. Things may not be as bad as they seem.*

86.4    **Dutch courage**
artificial courage resulting from drinking alcohol
*Before asking Freda to marry him, he got some **Dutch courage** by drinking a large glass of whisky.*

86.5    **have the nerve to**
have the (foolish) boldness to
*I don't know how you **have the nerve to** criticise Ted for being forgetful. Only a few days ago you forgot your own telephone number!*

## 87. FEAR

87.1    **have** one's **heart in** one's **boots**
feel frightened and depressed
***My heart was in my boots**. I was lost in the jungle, and I didn't see how anyone could ever find me.*

87.2    **have** one's **heart in** one's **mouth**
feel anxious or afraid
*Andrea's **heart was in her mouth** when her boy-friend drove his car too fast. She felt sure they would have an accident.*

87.3    **get the wind up**
become nervous and anxious
*When Jim noticed the two men behind him he **got the wind up**. He thought they were going to attack him.*

87.4    **jump out of** one's **skin**
get a great fright or shock (usually by a sudden movement or action)
*I nearly **jumped out of my skin** when you dropped that tray: it made such a loud noise.*

87.5 **in a cold sweat**
   very frightened, terrified
   *When I was in bed last night, I thought I heard a burglar downstairs and I broke out **in a cold sweat**.*

87.6 **frighten the life out** of someone
   **scare the hell out** of someone [!]
   **scare the pants** off someone [!]
   terrify someone
   *It **scared the hell out of/frightened the life out of/scared the pants off** James when his horse began to gallop. He was certain he'd fall off.*

87.7 **send chills up and down** someone's **spine**
   frighten someone
   *It **sent chills up and down** Karen's **spine** when she walked along the top of the wall. She thought she'd fall off.*

87.8 **make** someone's **flesh creep/crawl**
   make someone very frightened indeed
   *Some of these horror films are so frightening that they **make my flesh creep**.*

87.9 **make** someone's **hair stand on end**
   terrify someone, make him/her very frightened
   *The sound of the door opening in the middle of the night **made** Dave's **hair stand on end**.*

87.10 **put the wind up** someone
   make someone nervous and anxious
   *They said the police were coming to arrest me. That really **put the wind up** me!*

87.11 **have a yellow streak**
   be cowardly, lack courage
   *Tom **had a yellow streak** in him. He didn't want to help his friends to fight the gang from the next village.*

## 88. WILLINGNESS

88.1 **give** one's **right arm for** something
   be willing to do anything (to get something)
   *I'd **give my right arm for** a good job like Tom's.*

88.2 **fall over** oneself
   be keen to do everything possible (usually to help someone)
   *Philip was **falling over himself** to please Jane. He bought her bunches of flowers and several expensive presents.*

88.3 **a willing horse**
   a keen and willing worker
   *Robert is **a willing horse** and I know he'll try his best to do all the work we give him.*

88.4 **in the mood**
   ready and willing to do something
   *I'll do that job when I'm **in the mood**. I can work much faster when I'm ready and feel like it.*

88.5 **at the drop of a hat**
   willingly and immediately
   *He's prepared to go anywhere and do anything **at the drop of a hat**.*

88.6  **like a shot**
very willingly, quickly, eagerly
*I'd really like to get that job. If I'm offered it, I'll take it **like a shot**.*

88.7  **No sooner said than done.**
It will be done immediately. (used to show willingness)
*Carol asked Henry to drive her into town. "**No sooner said than done**," he replied, and they set off immediately.*

## 89. UNWILLINGNESS

89.1  **have no stomach for** doing something
be unwilling to do something, not determined or brave enough to do something
*Geoffrey **had no stomach for** rock climbing. He thought it was much too dangerous.*

89.2  **drag** one's **feet/heels**
do something slowly and unwillingly or without enthusiasm
*The government was **dragging its feet** about introducing the new proposal because a lot of people were opposed to it.*

89.3  **stop short of** doing something
be unwilling to go so far as to do something
*I know that Harry is dishonest but I'm sure he would **stop short of** committing a serious crime.*

89.4  **get blood out of a stone**
try to get something from someone who is very unwilling to give it
*Getting money from Simon is like **getting blood out of a stone**: he just will not pay.*

## 90. PRIDE

90.1  **get above** oneself
become too proud, start having too high an opinion of oneself
*Since her parents moved into a large flat, Priscilla has **got above** herself and no longer speaks to many of her old friends.*

90.2  **give** oneself **airs**
behave as if one is more important than one really is
*Ever since her husband was promoted to manager, Janet has **given herself airs**.*

90.3  **stand on** one's **dignity**
insist on being treated in the way one feels one deserves
*Although he is only a minor official, Mr Small **stands on his dignity** and insists on special treatment.*

90.4  **be/get on** one's **high horse**
act/begin to act in a proud manner so that one is difficult to talk to
*Henry thinks he is always right and **gets on his high horse** if anyone dares to contradict him.*

90.5  **keep up with the Joneses**
try to remain equal socially with one's neighbours, friends, etc., get the same things as they have
*Lucy's neighbour bought a new car, and so Lucy bought a new car, too. It was a case of **keeping up with the Joneses**.*

**90.6** **hold** one's **head high**
not feel ashamed (especially after a misfortune), feel (justly) proud
*Although Jimmy lost the tennis final, he can **hold his head high** because he put up a good fight.*

**90.7** **walk tall**
act proudly and not be ashamed of oneself
*Don't pay any attention if people laugh at you. **Walk tall** and show them you don't care.*

**90.8** **save face**
keep one's pride, avoid losing the respect of others
*When the Jacksons refused Tony's invitation to his party, he tried to **save face** among his friends by pretending he had not invited them.*

**90.9** **too big for** one's **boots**
too proud and conceited
*John is getting **too big for his boots** and wants people to think he is more important than he really is.*

**90.10** **put on airs and graces**
act unnaturally to show that one is very important, act proudly
*I don't know why Claire **puts on airs and graces**. After all, she has no reason to be so proud of herself.*

**90.11** **with** one's **nose in the air**
in a proud and scornful way, ignoring someone
*Ted didn't want to be seen with the poor old man and walked past him **with his nose in the air**.*

**90.12** **a clever dick/Dick** ⚠
**a smart alec/Alec** ⚠
a clever and conceited person
*John is such **a clever dick** nowadays. I don't know why he thinks he knows everything: he makes so many mistakes.*

**90.13** **a stuffed shirt**
a proud person who acts as if he is very important (and who lacks a sense of humour)
*Your neighbour's a bit of **a stuffed shirt**. He seems very proud and serious, and he never smiles or jokes with anyone.*

## 91. HUMILITY

**91.1** **bow and scrape**
behave very humbly, show (too) great respect
*Mr Robinson was **bowing and scraping** to everyone when the visitors came to inspect the factory.*

**91.2** **throw** oneself **at the feet of** someone
behave in a very humble way, beg for mercy
*The prisoner decided to **throw himself at the feet of** the judge and hoped that he would not be punished too severely.*

**91.3** **swallow** one's **pride**
act in a humble way, forget about pride
*Lionel can no longer afford an expensive car. He will simply have to **swallow his pride** and buy a cheaper one.*

**91.4** **take/bring** someone **down a peg or two**
make a proud person more humble or less important
*William thinks he is very important but he'll be **taken down a peg or two** when he goes into the Army.*

**91.5** **cut** someone **down to size**
make a proud person as humble as he/she ought to be
*It's time Harold was **cut down to size**. He's far too proud and conceited.*

**91.6** **take the wind out of** someone's **sails**
make someone who is over-confident feel less confident or even silly
*Ben was sure that Sheila would agree to marry him. Consequently, when she refused him, it **took the wind out of his sails**.*

**91.7** **lose face**
lose the respect of others
*The goal-keeper **lost face** by being dropped from the first team.*

**91.8** **cap in hand**
very humbly
*Mr Rumbelow couldn't get a new job and eventually had to go **cap in hand** to his old employer to get his job back.*

## 92. SATISFACTION

**92.1** **count** one's **blessings**
be grateful for what one has and for one's good fortune (instead of being unhappy about one's misfortunes, etc.)
*Arthur should **count his blessings**: he may not have a high salary but at least he has a nice wife and three lovely children.*

**92.2** **give** someone **a good run for their money**
compete well against someone, make an opponent work (or play) hard for success
*Although James didn't beat the champion, he played very well against him and **gave him a good run for his money**.*

## 93. DISSATISFACTION

**93.1** **get no change out of** someone
not get any help or satisfaction from someone
*I **got no change out of** the garage when I complained about the repairs to my car. They said the work had been done properly.*

**93.2** **leave a lot/much/a great deal/something to be desired**
used to express a feeling of dissatisfaction
*The orchestra was not very good and their performance left a **lot to be desired**.*

## 94. SURPRISE

**94.1** **not believe** one's **eyes/ears**
be so surprised or shocked that one cannot believe something one has seen/heard
*Dorothy **couldn't believe her ears** when Jane told her she was going to get married.*

94.2 **raise an eyebrow/raise (several, etc.) eyebrows**
cause surprise and unspoken disapproval
*When Ann wore her short dress at the party, she **raised several eyebrows**.*

94.3 **catch** someone **napping/catch** someone **on the wrong foot**
**catch** someone **on the hop**
surprise someone by occurring or causing to happen at an unexpected time (and not allowing preparation)
*Our firm was **caught napping/caught on the hop** when the new computers were delivered much earlier than expected. We were not ready to install them.*

94.4 **give** someone **a turn**
give someone a sudden shock or surprise
*You did **give me a turn** by speaking to me when I didn't know you were there.*

94.5 **take** someone's **breath away**
surprise or amaze someone
*It **took my breath away** when I learnt that John had left me £10,000 in his will. I had not expected anything.*

94.6 **The mind boggles at** something
It is hard to understand, believe or imagine (something)
***The mind boggles at** the great distance of the farthest stars in the universe.*

94.7 someone's **eyes almost/nearly popped out of his/her head**
used to indicate that someone was very surprised indeed
*Sheila's **eyes nearly popped out of her head** when her husband returned home unexpectedly.*

94.8 **(come) out of the blue**
(occur) unexpected(ly), without warning
*The news that I had won the competition **came out of the blue** because I had forgotten all about it.*

94.9 **a bolt out of/from the blue**
a sudden and unexpected piece of news, event, etc.
*The news that the boat had sunk came like **a bolt from the blue**. It was such a large boat, and the sea had been so calm.*

94.10 **a turn-up for the book(s)**
something (pleasant) which is unexpected or surprising
*So Fiona won the long jump? That's a **turn-up for the book**. It's the first time a girl from this school has won it.*

94.11 **Look what the cat's brought in!** [ ! ]
used humorously to show surprise at someone's arrival
*Well, Well! **Look what the cat's brought in!** Here's Jim, back from his holiday.*

94.12 **How about that?**
used to show astonishment or admiration
*Well, **how about that?** I never expected you to pass the test.*

94.13 **Come off it!**
often used to show surprise and angry disbelief at something said to one
***Come off it!** You don't expect us to believe such an unlikely story, do you?*

94.14 **(Well), did you ever!/(Well), I never did!**
used to show great surprise
***Well, I never did!** The man who was last at the beginning of the race has won it!*

**94.15 You don't say!**
used to show surprise and possibly disbelief at something said to one
*You don't say! I never expected to hear that Maureen had left her husband.*

**94.16 How can/could you!**
used to show surprise and disapproval
*Did you really tell them about my illness? How could you! It's a private matter.*

**94.17 Good heavens/God/Lord!** ⚠️
used to show surprise
*Good heavens! I would never have believed Dick could jump as high as that!*

**94.18 For heaven's/goodness' sake!**
**For God's sake!** ⚠️
used to show surprise and annoyance (Note that *for Christ's sake* is not used in polite conversation.)
*For heaven's sake, wake up and get dressed; you'll be late for school.*

**94.19 The (very) idea!**
used to show surprise and anger at something said
*The very idea! What you are saying is quite wrong.*

**94.20 Well, I like that!**
used sarcastically to show surprise and annoyance
*Well, I like that! After all I have done for him, how can he say I haven't helped him!*

**94.21 if you please**
used to show surprise or annoyance
*I finished that job a week earlier than expected and was told, if you please, that I had taken too long.*

**94.22 Stone me!**
used to show surprise
*Stone me! It's George! Who would have expected to see him here?*

**94.23 Well, I'll be blowed!/Blow me!**
used to show surprise and often anger
*You're really going without us! Well, I'll be blowed!*

**94.24 Words fail me!**
I cannot express my surprise/shock. (rather formal)
*Words fail me! I cannot describe how shocked I am by the statements put forward by the last speaker.*

**94.25 We live and learn!**
used to show surprise on hearing some news or information
*This article says that all the continents of the world were once joined together. Well, we live and learn.*

**94.26 a doubting Thomas**
someone who does not believe something unless he sees it for himself or has clear proof of it.
*You are a doubting Thomas. Must I prove absolutely everything to you before you believe me?*

**94.27 not bat an eyelid**
show no surprise at all
*Susie did not bat an eyelid when she heard that she'd lost money on a business deal. Perhaps she's so rich it didn't matter to her.*

## 95. SUSPICION

95.1 **something tells me**
I suspect that
*Something tells me that you already know who the thief was.*

95.2 **smell a rat**
become suspicious (that something is wrong)
*The insurance company smelt a rat when they looked into Mr Wright's claim. On further examination, they found that he had been lying about the true value of the stolen property.*

95.3 **under a cloud**
under suspicion, believed to have done something bad
*James left his job under a cloud. People said he had been dismissed for dishonesty, although it was never actually proved.*

95.4 **What's the/your game?/What's the big idea?** [!]
What are you doing? (used in surprise or anger; impolite)
*What's the big idea? Are you suggesting that I committed the crime?*

## 96. TELLING, REVEALING

96.1 **Get a load of this!** [!]
Listen to this! Look at this!
*Get a load of this! It says in the newspapers that Betty Wilson is getting married for the seventh time.*

96.2 **Spit it out!** [!]
Say what you want to/have to say! (usually used in the imperative to an inferior or a friend)
*Don't hesitate! Come on, spit it out! I want to hear what you have to say!*

96.3 **get something off one's chest**
talk about a problem or worry and thus get rid of it
*Would you like to tell me about your problem? You might feel better if you get it off your chest.*

96.4 **a word in someone's ear**
something said secretly or in confidence to someone
*William promised to have a word in the manager's ear and persuade him to give the order to his uncle.*

96.5 **let something slip**
tell something without intending to, reveal a secret unintentionally
*When Mary was talking to me, she let it slip that she didn't think much of Jimmy.*

96.6 **spill the beans**
reveal something, give away a secret
*Spill the beans and tell me all you know about Sandra and Philip.*

96.7 **let the cat out of the bag**
reveal a secret (sometimes unintentionally)
*We had meant to surprise Mary by giving her an expensive present for her birthday. However, my husband let the cat out of the bag and told her what it was.*

96.8 **blow the gaff**
reveal secrets about some dishonest or criminal act
*When he was arrested, he blew the gaff on the other thieves and told the police who they were.*

**96.9   blow** something **wide open**

make something widely known (often in a case under investigation by the police)

*This morning's newspaper article has **blown** the Smith affair **wide open**. Now everybody knows about it.*

**96.10   give the game away**

reveal a secret (usually unintentionally)

*If you tell them the principle of your new invention, you'll **give the game away** and everyone will copy it.*

**96.11   put** one's **foot in it**

reveal or say something offensive or embarrassing without intending to do so.

*I'm afraid I **put my foot in it** when I said that I'd seen David with his girlfriend. I didn't know he was married.*

**96.12   a slip of the tongue**

something said or revealed by mistake when the speaker intended to say something else

*I didn't mean to say that there was a profit of £2,000. It was **a slip of the tongue**: the profit was only £200.*

**96.13   say** one's **piece**

say what one has planned to say

*I know you've been wanting to speak to us. So **say your piece**, and tell us what you think should be done.*

**96.14   have** one's **say**

have one's turn at saying what one thinks

*Well, you've **had your say**. Now be quiet and let someone else speak.*

**96.15   to** someone's **face**

(said) directly and frankly to someone

*I'm not afraid of him. I'll tell him **to his face** what I think of him.*

**96.16   talk nineteen to the dozen**

talk a lot, usually very quickly

*Bob's a real talker! He **talks nineteen to the dozen**. I get tired of listening to him.*

**96.17   talk shop**

talk about details connected with one's work (especially in a setting outside one's work)

*Please excuse us for **talking shop**. We find it hard to stop thinking about our work, even at weekends.*

**96.18   can talk the hind legs off a donkey/mule**

talks too much (often used in a derogatory way)

*That salesman **can talk the hind legs off a donkey** and it's hard even to ask him any questions: he simply never stops.*

**96.19   for the record**

for the purpose of what is written in an official record (of a meeting, etc.); a deliberate statement

***For the record**, I wish to make it clear that I do not agree with the decision just taken by the committee.*

**96.20   go on record**

be reported accurately and according to one's wishes (about something

one says), make one's attitude clear
*I want to go on record as saying that I do not know the man who has accused me.*

96.21 **off the record**
unofficially, not to be repeated or reported in writing
*Off the record, I do not really support the government's policy, but I do not wish to be quoted as saying so.*

96.22 **with** one's **tongue in** one's **cheek**
said in a way which is not meant to be taken seriously
*Tina said she adored James and loved getting telephone calls from him. But I know she was speaking with her tongue in her cheek. She doesn't like him at all.*

96.23 **stop beating/not beat about the bush**
be/start being absolutely clear and direct in what one says
*Stop beating about the bush and tell me what is really wrong.*

96.24 **find** one's **tongue**
begin to talk (after being quiet)
*Haven't you found your tongue yet? Why don't you say something?*

96.25 **to cut a long story short**
to speak briefly (and omit irrelevant details)
*. . . well, to cut a long story short, I eventually found the shop but it was closed!*


## 97. KEEPING QUIET, NOT TELLING

97.1 **keep** something **dark/keep** something **under** one's **hat**
keep something a secret
*Keep it dark./Keep it under your hat. I don't want anyone else to know what I've told you.*

97.2 **keep mum about** something
keep quiet about something
*Tim kept mum about his new job, didn't he? I didn't even know he had started.*

97.3 **on the quiet/sly**
secretly
*Freda told me on the quiet that Bill had asked her to marry him.*

97.4 **play/hold/keep** one's **cards close to** one's **chest**
keep things secret, not reveal much
*It's difficult to know what John is going to do. He plays his cards close to his chest.*

97.5 **My lips are sealed.**
I shan't tell anyone. (If someone's lips are sealed, they have agreed to keep something a secret.)
*My lips are sealed and I won't tell anybody what you are going to do.*

97.6 **Mum's the word!**
Don't tell anyone!
*I don't want you to tell anyone that I'm applying for a new job. Mum's the word!*

97.7 **Put a sock in it!** ⚠
Stop talking and be quiet!
*Put a sock in it and stop talking. We're all tired of listening to you.*

97.8 **not get a word in edgeways**
not be able to speak because another person is talking too much
*Harry talked so much that no one else could get a word in edgeways.*

## 98. DISCUSSING, ARGUING

98.1 **put our/your/their heads together**
discuss something together
*Let's **put our heads together** and try to solve this problem.*

98.2 **have it out with** someone
have a frank discussion with someone to settle an argument or quarrel
*I'm going to see Frank and **have it out with** him. It's time we knew what he's doing.*

98.3 **have words with** someone
have an argument or quarrel with someone
*I'm afraid I've just **had words with** Kate: I didn't think she should have left the meeting.*

98.4 **argue the toss** $\boxed{!}$
argue about something which cannot be changed, question a decision which has been made
*You're always **arguing the toss**. Why can't you just accept what we've decided and help us to do it?*

98.5 **cross swords with** someone
argue, come near to quarrelling (with someone)
*John **crossed swords with** Patrick when he told him he didn't believe a word he said.*

98.6 **take issue with** someone
argue/disagree with someone
*I'll **take issue with** you on that subject. I don't agree with you at all.*

98.7 **be at it**
be arguing, quarrelling, etc. (when this happens repeatedly)
*They're **at it** again — arguing, as usual!*

98.8 **after/when all is said and done**
taking everything into consideration, looking at the complete situation
***When all is said and done**, they should have treated the old man with much more respect.*

98.9 **get down to brass tacks**
begin to talk about the important facts in a situation
*We have talked about replacing this machine for a long time, but we must now **get down to brass tacks** and decide what type to buy.*

98.10 **(have) the last/final word**
(make) the final statement in an argument
*Bill will insist on **having the last word**. He can't bear to lose an argument.*

98.11 **be/talk at cross-purposes**
have a conversation in which one person misunderstands the other person
*We were **talking at cross-purposes**: I wanted to know the company's plans for next year, and he thought I wanted to change those plans.*

98.12 **eat** one's **words**
admit that what one said previously is wrong
*Several people quoted facts to prove that Harry was wrong, and he had to **eat his words**.*

98.13 **a running battle/fight**
an argument or dispute which continues over a period of time
*Sam and his wife had **a running battle** over whether they should buy a new cooker. Sam didn't want to get one but his wife did.*

98.14 **cut and thrust**
vigorous argument, fierce competition, attack and counter-attack
*There is a lot of **cut and thrust** in the market these days. The competition for business is very fierce.*

98.15 **(weigh up) the pros and cons**
(consider) the arguments for and against something
*I shall **weigh up the pros and cons** of the situation before deciding what to do.*

98.16 **in question**
being discussed, mentioned, referred to
*The proposals **in question** needn't be discussed today: they can be left until next week.*

98.17 **cut the cackle** ⚠
stop talking about superficial things and begin a serious discussion or argument
***Cut the cackle**, James! It's time you talked more seriously.*

98.18 **shift** one's **ground**
change one's arguments
*It's difficult to argue with Jonathan — he's constantly **shifting his ground**.*

98.19 **go round in circles**
repeat one's arguments without reaching agreement
*We'll never reach an agreement: we're just **going round in circles**.*

98.20 **flog** something **to death**
discuss something so much that it is no longer of any interest
*Let's change the subject and talk about something else. We've **flogged** this topic **to death**.*


## 99. AGREEING

99.1 **of one mind/of the same mind**
in total agreement
*We found we were **of one mind** and could both vote in the same way.*

99.2 **at one**
in complete agreement
*The two prime ministers discussed the matter and found they were **at one**: both wanted to avoid a trade war at any cost.*

99.3 **in tune with** someone/something
in agreement with someone/something
*Dick Jones is very much **in tune with** his boss and knows exactly what she wants.*

99.4 **go all the way**
agree completely
*I **go all the way** with your suggestion that we provide you with an assistant. You have too much work to do.*

**99.5 see eye to eye** (with someone)

be in (complete) agreement (often used in the negative to show disagreement)

*John wants to do one thing and James another; they **don't see eye to eye** on most things.*

**99.6 give the O.K./okay/go-ahead**

agree, consent

*David Lowe **gave the O.K.** for us to start the job.*

**99.7 take** someone's **point**

agree (in a limited way) with someone, accept the truth of what they have said (about a certain point only)

*I **take** your **point** about the poor working conditions in the office. However, I'm afraid there's no more money to improve them.*

**99.8 come to terms with** someone

reach an agreement with someone

*The men have **come to terms with** their employers and the strike is over.*

**99.9 Hear! Hear!**

I agree (used to show agreement with a public speaker)

*There were loud calls of "**Hear! Hear!**" as the audience showed its approval of the speaker's remarks.*

**99.10 Quite so!**

used to show agreement with what someone has just said

***Quite so!** I entirely agree with what you say.*

**99.11 I don't blame you**

I agree; I think you're right.

*"I was so angry that I left at once." "**I don't blame you**. I'd have done the same."*

**99.12 Right you are!**

used to show willingness or agreement

***Right you are!** We'll take this path, as you suggest.*

**99.13 Fair enough!**

used to show agreement that something is reasonable

*"I'll help you only if you promise to help me." "**Fair enough!**"*

**99.14 You can say that again!/You're telling me!**

used to show strong agreement and support of something said

***You can say that again!/You're telling me!** It's a view I have always held.*

**99.15 Now you're talking!**

Now I agree. (used to encourage someone)

***Now you're talking!** At last, we can make some progress.*

**99.16 Too true/right!**

Certainly! (used to show agreement, also sometimes used regretfully)

***Too true;** you're quite right in what you say, though I wish it were not so.*

**99.17 You've said it!/You said it!**

Certainly! (used to show strong agreement)

***You've said it!** I couldn't agree with you more!*

**99.18 sign on the dotted line**

sign a written agreement

***Sign on the dotted line** if you want to hire the car.*

99.19 **split the difference**
agree on a compromise, usually an amount of money half way between the two amounts being discussed
*You say it's worth £5 and I say £3. Shall we **split the difference** and make it £4?*

99.20 **pay lip service to** something
support something in what one says, but not in what one really thinks nor in one's actions
*Mr Lawson only **pays lip service to** the idea of sharing profits equally — but, in fact, he takes as much for himself as he can.*

## 100. DISAGREEING

100.1 **at odds with** someone
in disagreement with someone
*I'm **at odds with** my boyfriend because I dared to say I didn't like his new car.*

100.2 **at loggerheads** (with someone)
in disagreement with someone, in a state of mutual hostility
*The company and the trade union are **at loggerheads** over working conditions in the factory.*

100.3 **make something out of** something
disagree or even fight
*You are trying to **make something out of** what I said. Forget it: it's very unimportant.*

100.4 **agree to differ**
agree not to argue further because there is no hope of agreeing
*Very well! Neither of us will change our mind, so let's **agree to differ**.*

100.5 **have an/no axe to grind**
have a/no personal reason for doing something (usually something which causes disagreement)
*I only want to help you to find the best solution to your problem. I **have no axe to grind** and it will not benefit me in any way.*

100.6 **a bone of contention**
a cause of disagreement or argument
*Whether he should see his friends every night is **a bone of contention** between Joe and his wife.*

100.7 **If you think that/etc., you've got another think coming (to you)!** [!]
What you think is going to happen will not happen.
*If you think I'm going to swim across this river, **you've got another think coming**: I'm not.*

100.8 **Far from it!/Nothing of the kind!**
used to show strong disagreement with a statement made
*"I think Louise is rather lazy." "**Far from it!/Nothing of the kind!** She works very hard indeed."*

## 101. EATING, DRINKING

101.1 **make** one's **mouth water**
make one want to have something (especially food)
*Those peaches look so good that they **make my mouth water**.*

101.2  **make a pig of** oneself
eat or drink too much
*The doctor told me to have light meals only, and so I mustn't **make a pig of myself.***

101.3  **on the house**
free of charge (usually used about food and drinks in restaurants and bars)
*These drinks are **on the house**. It's the restaurant's tenth anniversary.*

101.4  **drink like a fish**
regularly drink a lot of alcohol
*Cyril **drinks like a fish** and usually has at least six glasses of beer every evening.*

101.5  **hit the bottle**
begin to drink a lot of alcohol regularly
*I'm afraid Mark is **hitting the bottle** quite a lot these days. He'll ruin his health if he continues to drink like that.*

101.6  **have one over the eight**
have too much to drink, get drunk
*David has **had one over the eight** and shouldn't be allowed to drive his car.*

101.7  **drown** one's **sorrows**
try to escape one's troubles by drinking alcohol
*He was very upset when he lost his job, and so he **drowned his sorrows** in whisky.*

101.8  **as drunk as a lord**
very drunk
*George is **as drunk as a lord** — he has been drinking beer all evening.*

101.9  **under the influence**
drunk
*The policeman said that George was driving from one side of the road to the other and was clearly **under the influence**.*

101.10  **the worse for wear**
drunk (or tired, or unwell)
*The man had been drinking in the bar all day and was very much **the worse for wear**.*

101.11  **a hair of the dog (that bit** one)
a small drink of alcohol taken after one has drunk too much (and supposed to act as a cure), usually on the following day
*What about **a hair of the dog**? It'll make us both feel better after last night's party.*

101.12  **on the wagon**
intending not to drink any alcohol at all
*I'm **on the wagon** because the doctor told me not to drink any more.*

101.13  **on the rocks**
on small pieces of ice (used only in connection with alcoholic drinks)
*"Do you like ice in your whisky?" "Yes, whisky **on the rocks**, please."*

## 102. SPENDING MONEY

102.1  **change hands**
be sold or given by one person to another, pass from one to another
*This car has **changed hands** so many times that there must be something wrong with it.*

102.2 **sell/go like hot cakes**
be sold or taken very quickly
*That new toy will **sell like hot cakes**, especially at such a low price.*

102.3 **foot the bill**
pay the bill
*John told his wife to get the new dress she wanted and said that he would **foot the bill**.*

102.4 **hold the purse-strings**
control the supply of money, be in charge of the money
*James's wife **holds the purse-strings**: she pays all the bills and just gives him an allowance.*

102.5 **out of pocket**
having spent or lost some money
*The shopkeeper said he was **out of pocket** on these computers. He had to sell them for less than he paid for them.*

102.6 **on tick**
with a promise to pay later, on credit
*Judith has an account at that shop and so she gets everything **on tick**.*

102.7 **pay** one's **way**
earn enough to pay one's expenses
*The rent for these shops is now so high that they no longer **pay their way**. They cost a lot to run but don't bring in much money.*

# 103. COST

103.1 **cost/pay the earth**
cost/pay a lot of money
*I can't possibly afford to buy a camera like Ted's. It **costs the earth**.*

103.2 **cost/make/spend/lose a packet**
cost/make/spend/lose a lot of money
*I **lost a packet** on that race. The horse I bet on came in last!*

103.3 **Money/expense is no object.**
It doesn't matter how much it costs.
***Money is no object**. Spend what you like on your new computer if it is really what you need.*

103.4 **over the odds**
more than expected, more than the official price
*These new computers are in short supply, and you have to pay **over the odds** to get one.*

103.5 **cost a pretty penny**
cost a lot of money
*A good video camera will **cost** you **a pretty penny**.*

103.6 **daylight/highway robbery**
far more expensive than it should be
*That's **highway robbery**! I can buy the same thing for half the price at the shop down the road!*

103.7 **cut** one's **coat according to** one's **cloth**
do only what is possible with the money or resources available
*I'm afraid we can't afford to buy a big car. We'll just have to cut our coat according to our cloth and buy a small one.*

103.8 **spoil the ship for a halfpennyworth/ha'porth o' tar**
spoil something valuable by not spending enough money on small but necessary improvements, maintenance, etc.
*He spoiled the ship for a ha'porth o' tar when he had his lorry repainted — a much better job could have been done for very little extra money.*

103.9 **on a shoestring**
without spending much money, very cheaply
*John runs his shop on a shoestring and spends very little on new stock.*

103.10 **for a song**
very cheaply indeed
*I bought that old Chinese vase for a song. I expected to pay much more.*

103.11 **ten a penny**
cheap, abundant, common
*Pieces of jewellery like that are ten a penny. You can buy them in any large department store.*

## 104. WEALTH

104.1 **in the money**
rich (after being quite poor)
*Now I'm in the money — I've just won the football pools!*

104.2 **well off**
rich
*Henry is very well off: he's got a well-paid job and a very nice house.*

104.3 **well-to-do**
rich
*They're quite a well-to-do family. They have two expensive cars and a big house.*

104.4 **be rolling in it**
be extremely rich
*Harriet must be rolling in it. She has had four husbands, and they each left her a lot of money when they died.*

104.5 **have/with money to burn**
have/with so much money that one needn't worry how much one spends
*John must have money to burn if he can buy all these expensive electrical gadgets.*

104.6 **make** one's **pile**
make a lot of money
*Mr Jones made his pile out of selling second-hand cars. He's now got several men working for him.*

104.7 **strike it rich**
suddenly earn a lot of money, become rich
*Jake Simpson struck it rich with the last book he wrote. It was an immediate best-seller.*

104.8   **feather** one's **own nest**
       make money for oneself (especially by corrupt actions)
       *The corrupt government officer used public money to feather his own nest.*
104.9   **have an easy time of it**
       have a comfortable life and a lot of money, etc.
       *Bob has an easy time of it: he has plenty of money and never has to work.*
104.10  **They've/We've/etc. never had it so good.**
       They/We/etc. are more comfortable and prosperous than ever before.
       *The people of that country have never had it so good: there is full employment and almost everyone has a nice home.*
104.11  **in the lap of luxury**
       leading a very comfortable life, wealthy
       *When I last saw Henry, he was living in London in the lap of luxury. He seemed to have everything he could wish for.*
104.12  **when someone's ship comes in/home**
       when someone eventually becomes very rich
       *I'll buy a nice house and a new car when my ship comes in.*
104.13  **keep the wolf from the door**
       get enough to stay alive, and avoid hunger (often used humorously)
       *I don't earn much — only just enough to keep the wolf from the door.*
104.14  **keep** one's **head above water**
       stay out of debt
       *Helen keeps her head above water by working long hours.*
104.15  **make (both) ends meet**
       not spend more than one earns
       *The only way to make both ends meet is to keep your expenses below the level of your earnings.*
104.16  **from rags to riches**
       from poverty to wealth
       *Harry Lee has gone from rags to riches: he started work as an office boy and is now a manager.*
104.17  **the haves and the have-nots**
       those who are rich and those who are poor
       *There is still great bitterness between the haves and the have-nots in many countries today, especially as a result of the high unemployment rate.*

## 105. POVERTY

105.1   **not have a bean**
       not have any money at all
       *I can't afford to buy a cup of tea. I haven't a bean!*
105.2   **not have a penny to** one's **name**
       have no money at all
       *I'd get a small car if I had some money but I haven't a penny to my name.*
105.3   **live from hand to mouth**
       be very poor, spend all the money one gets immediately, simply to stay alive
       *I was living from hand to mouth and I even had to clean a friend's flat every week to pay the bills.*

**105.4 in queer street**
in financial difficulty
*Don't accept a cheque from Bob. He's **in queer street** and the bank will not accept any cheque he signs.*

**105.5 down and out**
unemployed, homeless, without any money
*The poor old man has no job and is completely **down and out**.*

**105.6 in the red**
owing money (usually to one's bank), in debt
*I've just got my bank statement and I'm afraid I'm **in the red**. I've overspent by £50.*

**105.7 hard up**
not having much money
*Can you lend me some money for a cup of coffee? I'm rather **hard up** at present.*

**105.8 feel the pinch/draught**
suffer because of lack of money
*Shopkeepers are beginning to **feel the pinch** because no one has a lot of money to spend these days.*

**105.9 not made of money**
not having a lot of money (often used in reply to requests for money)
*I'm **not made of money**! I can't afford to lend you money to buy a car.*

**105.10 rough it**
live a hard and uncomfortable life, be poor
*When Mr Low was a student, he had to **rough it**, but now he lives very comfortably.*

**105.11 down at heel**
poor, untidy
*Harry Bright looked very **down at heel** when I last saw him: he was wearing an old coat, and was dirty and unshaven.*

## 106. GENERAL BEHAVIOUR

**106.1 mend** one's **ways/manners**
improve one's behaviour
*You'll have to **mend your ways** if you want to be successful in your job.*

**106.2 not put a foot wrong**
behave absolutely correctly, behave very well
*John made a good impression on everyone: he **never put a foot wrong**.*

**106.3 have a way with** one
have a charming and attractive manner
*Harry **has a way with him** and seems to attract lots of beautiful girls.*

**106.4 kick over the traces**
oppose the rules which had controlled one
*Lolita got tired of her strict life at home, and so she **kicked over the traces** and settled in a different town.*

**106.5 turn over a new leaf**
reform, begin to behave in a much better way
*His army service has done John a great deal of good: he has **turned over a new leaf** and is behaving much better than he did.*

106.6 **come out of** one's **shell**
become more confident, less shy
*Since he left school, and took a job, Peter has **come out of his shell** and is no longer shy.*

106.7 **try it on**
behave badly in order to find out what will be allowed
*When they have a new teacher, the boys always **try it on**.*

106.8 **make an exhibition of** oneself
behave in a foolish way in public
*Stop **making an exhibition of yourself** and control your temper.*

106.9 **draw the line at** something
set limits on how one is prepared to behave
*I **draw the line at** singing a solo in public. I'll tell jokes but I won't sing.*

106.10 **be second nature to/with/for** someone
be part of one's normal habits, automatic behaviour
*It's **second nature with** him to check that all the lights are switched off whenever he leaves the office.*

106.11 **in character**
according to the way someone usually behaves
*I think William was the boy who played the trick on you. It would be quite **in character** — the sort of thing he usually does.*

106.12 **free and easy**
informal, not closely following any rules
*This hotel is **free and easy**. You can wear whatever you want in the restaurant.*

106.13 **beyond the pale**
outside the limits of normal good behaviour
*Jimmy is **beyond the pale**. There is nothing anyone can do to improve his behaviour.*

106.14 **one of the old school**
a person who has old ideas and attitudes
*Emma's father is **one of the old school**, and he always insists on wearing a tie.*

106.15 **like a bull in a china shop**
in a clumsy or rough way, without tact
*It's no use sending Tom to see any dissatisfied customers. He'll behave **like a bull in a china shop** and only offend everyone.*

106.16 **off-hand**
not caring about other people's feelings
*When I complained to the shop, the manager was very **off-hand** and just didn't want to hear what I had to say.*

106.17 **in cold blood**
deliberately, calmly and without emotion
*The murderer killed his victim **in cold blood**. He had carefully planned the murder several months before.*

106.18 **hail-fellow-well-met**
very friendly (from the moment of meeting)
*You'll find it easy to get on well with John. His **hail-fellow-well-met** attitude makes him easy to talk to.*

106.19  **not stand on ceremony**
not behave in a formal way
*Let's **not stand on ceremony** — call me by my first name.*

106.20  Someone's **bark is worse than his/her bite.**
Although someone sounds angry, he is not as bad-tempered and as
frightening as he appears at first.
*Bill loves to argue and shout a lot, but his **bark is worse than his bite** and he
doesn't mean all he says.*

106.21  **That's** someone **all over**
That's typical of someone
*Teddy never told anyone about his brave act in rescuing the little boy. **That's
Teddy all over** — he's very modest.*

## 107. EXPERIENCE

107.1  **see the world**
have a lot of experience, have travelled about a lot
*Vincent seems like a man who has **seen the world** and knows a lot about
everything.*

107.2  **an old hand**
someone with a lot of experience
*Philip is **an old hand** at repairing clocks. He has been doing it for many years.*

107.3  **a new one on** someone
be a new problem, idea, situation, etc. to someone
*That's **a new one on** me! I haven't heard that idea before.*

107.4  **(still) wet behind the ears**
inexperienced, young
*Johnny is **still wet behind the ears**; he's young and he's only been in this job a
short time.*

## 108. AGE

108.1  **feel/look/show** one's **age**
feel/seem/appear old (at least as old as one is)
*Jack is **looking his age** now since his illness last year.*

108.2  **have one foot in the grave**
be very old or ill, be almost dying
*My grandmother says she **has one foot in the grave**. She has been complaining
about her illnesses for years.*

108.3  **long in the tooth**
old (used in a rather derogatory or humorous way)
*John's getting a bit **long in the tooth** for discotheques!*

108.4  **have seen/known better days**
be no longer in good condition (because of age), be too old (used in a
derogatory way)
*The machinery **has seen better days**, and it is time to replace it.*

108.5  **past it** ⚠
too old (used in a rather derogatory way)
*Ann's really getting **past it** — she can't do a lot of the things she enjoyed when she
was younger.*

108.6 **on the shelf** $\boxed{!}$
unmarried and unlikely to get married because one is too old
*Nicola's been left **on the shelf** and is a bit old now to marry.*

108.7 **put/send/turn** someone **out to grass**
make someone finish working because he/she is old (usually used humorously)
*Perhaps the management would like to **put me out to grass**, but I'll stay on in this job for another year or two.*

108.8 **Darby and Joan**
any old couple who are happily married (usually used humorously)
*That old couple really are a **Darby and Joan**, happily married for over 60 years.*

108.9 **be/act** one's **age**
behave like an adult (and not like a child)
*You're eighteen now and it's time you **acted your age** and behaved properly.*

108.10 **fresh/new blood**
a new person in a group of people, bringing liveliness, new ideas, etc.
*We need some **new blood** in this company so that we can have some fresh ideas.*

108.11 **young at heart**
having a young, fresh outlook or attitude despite one's age (used to praise someone)
*Mr Lawson is nearly eighty, but he's still **young at heart** and interested in everything we do.*

## 109. HEALTH

109.1 **hale and hearty**
fit and cheerful, in very good health
*Lisa looked **hale and hearty** when I saw her today, and said she was feeling very fit.*

109.2 **alive and kicking**
alive and in good health, still active (especially after illness or danger to one's health)
*I thought James was ill in hospital but I saw him in town this morning, **alive and kicking**.*

109.3 **in the pink**
very well, in good health
*"How are you Philip?" "**In the pink**, thanks. I haven't felt better for a long time."*

109.4 **(not) be/feel** oneself
(not) feel healthy and/or happy
*Anne's much better today and says **she's** almost **herself** again.*

109.5 **still going strong**
still healthy, still getting along well
*Old Fred is **still going strong** and still working on his farm every day.*

109.6 **up and about**
fully recovered, out of bed
*Mabel has now fully recovered from her accident and is **up and about** again.*

109.7 **up and down**
sometimes well and sometimes unwell
*"How's your father?" "I'm afraid he's **up and down**. One day he seems to be all right and the next day he seems to be quite ill."*

## 110.  SICKNESS, EXHAUSTION

110.1  **not feel too/so hot**
not feel very well, feel rather ill
*I'm **not feeling so hot** this morning. I stayed up too late last night.*

110.2  **flaked out**
exhausted, very tired
*I'm **flaked out.** I must go to bed for a short time.*

110.3  **under the weather**
unwell, miserable
*Mary has been **under the weather** since her mother died.*

110.4  **out of sorts**
slightly unwell, in a bad mood
*I feel a bit **out of sorts** — I must have eaten something that was bad.*

110.5  **(all) washed out**
tired, without energy
*I'm **all washed out.** I haven't the energy to do anything at all.*

110.6  **all in**
exhausted, very tired
*I'm **all in** after the difficult climb up the mountain.*

110.7  **take to** one's **bed**
go to bed because one is ill
*I wasn't feeling very well and **took to my bed** for a couple of days. The rest did me a lot of good.*

110.8  **feel/look like death warmed up** ⚠
feel/appear very ill or tired
*Whatever have you been doing? You **look like death warmed up**!*

110.9  **catch** one's **death (of cold)**
catch a bad cold
*You'll **catch your death of cold** if you go out in this cold weather without your coat.*

110.10  **thin on top**
becoming bald, having little hair on one's head
*Peter has plenty of hair at the sides but is a bit **thin on top**.*

## 111.  DEATH

111.1  **kick the bucket** ⚠
die
*I want to enjoy life as long as I can before I **kick the bucket**.*

111.2  **give up the ghost**
die, be beyond repair (formal or religious for people; humorous for things)
*This machine has **given up the ghost**: it's impossible to repair it.*

111.3  **snuff it** ⚠
die
*Poor Peter looks as if he might **snuff it** any day. He's very ill indeed.*

111.4  **lay down** one's **life**
die (for one's country or others)
*My grandfather was one of the many people who **laid down their lives** for their country during the Second World War.*

111.5 someone's **number is up**
someone is going to die, suffer or be punished
*I hate flying, and I really thought my **number was up** when the plane made an emergency landing.*

111.6 **on** one's/its **last legs**
about to die or collapse from exhaustion, age, etc.
*This car is **on its last legs** and won't run much longer.*

111.7 **hang by a thread**
be in great danger, especially near death
*For some time after her dangerous operation, Karen's life **hung by a thread**.*

111.8 **lay** someone **to rest**
bury a dead person
*My grandmother died last week, and we **laid her to rest** today.*

111.9 **take** one's **life in** one's **hands**
risk being killed, risk having an accident
*Those acrobats at the circus **take their lives in their hands** during every performance. Their act is extremely dangerous.*

## 112. RUIN, HARM

112.1 **be all up with** someone
be ruined, be the end of someone
*It's **all up with** Terry Sharp. He's been arrested by the police.*

112.2 **gone for a burton/Burton**
ruined, killed, finished
*Joe's business has **gone for a Burton** because of lack of trade.*

112.3 **go to the dogs**
be ruined (through one's own fault), become worthless
*He's **gone to the dogs** since his wife divorced him. He's drinking far too much and he doesn't look after himself.*

112.4 **go to rack and ruin**
become useless or ruined, decay through neglect
*This building will **go to rack and ruin** unless it is repaired.*

112.5 **(all) washed up**
ruined, finished, defeated
*I'm **all washed up** — I've tried my best to succeed and I've failed.*

112.6 **on the rocks**
1 breaking up (used about a marriage)
*Tom and Betty's marriage is **on the rocks** because Tom's been going out with other women.*
2 becoming ruined as a result of lack of money (used about businesses)
*Eric's business really had no chance. It needed more money from the start and now it's **on the rocks**.*

112.7 **cook** one's **(own) goose**
do something to harm or ruin oneself
*Poor Frank **cooked his own goose** when he told the manager about his previous mistakes.*

**112.8**   **cut** one's **(own) throat**
act in such a way that one harms oneself, usually because of pride, etc.
*The shop is **cutting its own throat** by making all its goods far too expensive.*

**112.9**   **will be the death of** someone
will kill someone, by persisting in some action (sometimes used humorously)
*You'll **be the death of** me if you go on talking like that. You're so funny that I can't stop laughing.*

**112.10**   **bring** someone/something **to his/her/its knees**
bring someone/something close to ruin or defeat
*Business is terrible at the moment — the economic situation is **bringing** us **to our knees**.*

**112.11**   **drive/hammer a nail in(to)** one's **coffin**
do something to destroy one's health
*He drove another **nail into his coffin** by drinking a lot of beer, even though the doctor had told him not to drink any alcohol at all.*

**112.12**   **cut their own throats**
harm themselves, usually as a result of competition in business
*In time these two shopkeepers will **cut their own throats**. They're always reducing prices to obtain each other's trade.*

**112.13**   **make a dent/hole in** something
harm something (someone's reputation, profits, etc.)
*Fierce competition has **made a dent in** our profits this year. They are only half what they were last year.*

**112.14**   **get** one's **fingers burnt**
suffer because one has done something (or interfered in a matter) and failed
*Don't try to interfere in their marriage. You'll only **get your fingers burnt**.*

**112.15**   **lay** oneself **(wide) open** (to criticism, blame, attack, etc.)
put oneself in a position where one can be harmed
*If you publicly attack his policies, you'll **lay yourself wide open** to criticism from his supporters.*

**112.16**   **lay a finger on** someone
harm or threaten to harm someone (usually used in the negative)
*Don't **lay a finger on** David or I'll call the police.*

**112.17**   **the last straw/the straw that broke the camel's back**
a small additional difficulty which makes an unpleasant situation impossible to bear
*Nothing was going right for Elsie and she burst into tears when she burnt the cake. It was **the last straw**!*

## 113.   FAILURE, LOSS

**113.1**   **miss the boat/bus**
be too late to take advantage of an opportunity
*George **missed the boat/bus** when he did not buy this house last year: now the price has doubled.*

113.2 **let** something **slip through** one's **fingers**
fail to keep or obtain something one had the chance of having, lose an opportunity
*The football manager had a bad season last year. He let several talented young players slip through his fingers, and they joined other clubs.*

113.3 **go down the drain**
be completely wasted or lost
*All Mr Black's hard work went down the drain last year when his book was not accepted for publication.*

113.4 **have had** one's **chips** [!]
have failed, have been defeated (or be about to fail or be defeated)
*"Dave's been arrested by the police. I'm sure he'll be sent to prison." "Yes, I'm afraid he's had his chips".*

113.5 **come to grief**
fail, be destroyed, be damaged
*The racing driver came to grief at the start of the race when he collided with another car.*

113.6 **come to nothing**
fail, not result in anything
*All her good work came to nothing because her colleagues refused to help her.*

113.7 **fall by the wayside**
fail to continue, give up a struggle (usually because of exhaustion, lack of interest or discouragement)
*A lot of people fall by the wayside when writing a book: they give up because they eventually lose interest in it.*

113.8 **come down in the world**
fall to a lower social position, job, etc.
*George has come down in the world. He used to own three shops but now he drives an ice-cream van.*

113.9 **fall flat**
fail completely in its intended effect
*The comedian's jokes fell flat and no one laughed at all.*

113.10 **come off second best**
be beaten (in a competition, game, fight, etc.)
*The champion came off second best in tonight's match: his opponent won easily.*

113.11 **fight a losing battle**
struggle with little chance of success
*You'll be fighting a losing battle if you try to persuade Tina to change her mind. She's extremely stubborn.*

113.12 **back the wrong horse/a loser**
support the wrong person or cause (especially a loser)
*I'm afraid we backed the wrong horse in the elections. The candidate we supported came last.*

113.13 **at the expense of**
with the loss of
*The army eventually won the battle but only at the expense of several hundred men killed and wounded.*

113.14 **throw in the towel/the sponge**/one's **hand**
admit defeat, give up all hope of winning (especially in a competition)
*Henry could see he had no chance of winning the race. So he **threw in the towel**.*

113.15 **a lost cause**
something that is bound to fail
*He is supporting **a lost cause** — no one is interested any longer in his outdated ideas.*

## 114. SUCCESS, GAIN, WINNING

114.1 **make a go of it**/something
succeed, make something work
*I do hope that he **will make a go of** the new business he has just started — he deserves to succeed.*

114.2 **make** one's **mark**
be successful, become well-known
*Alison has **made her mark** in the theatre and is already playing leading parts.*

114.3 **make it**
succeed
*There is no doubt that this new footballer will **make it** because he has all the skills and knows how to use them.*

114.4 **make good**
be a success (usually after difficulties or failure)
*Robert had a poor start in life but in the end he **made good** and became very successful.*

114.5 **go up in the world**
rise to a higher social position, better job, etc.
*He's **gone up in the world** since I last saw him. Now he's got three cars and a big house!*

114.6 **(not)/set the world on fire**
(not) be very successful, (not) cause a sensation
*I'm sure she'll do very well — though she'll **never set the world on fire**.*

114.7 **fall/land on** one's **feet**
be successful or lucky (usually after having had a difficult time)
*Mary is very fortunate and always **lands on her feet** in spite of all the obstacles put in her way.*

114.8 **have a lot going for** one
be likely to succeed because there are a lot of things in one's favour
*Mary **has a lot going for** her; she is intelligent, attractive and a very talented pianist.*

114.9 **go with a bang/swing**
go successfully, very well
*The party **went with a bang/swing**, and everyone thoroughly enjoyed it.*

114.10 **have/got it made**
be sure of success
*Mr Robinson **has got it made** — his new business has proved very successful.*

**114.11  with flying colours**
with great success (and ease)
*Helen passed all her examinations **with flying colours** and has now got a good job with a computer firm.*

**114.12  (ride) on the crest of a wave**
(be) at a very successful point or stage
*Our company is now **riding on the crest of a wave**, and business has improved rapidly.*

**114.13  on the up and up**
becoming more and more successful, improving
*Mr Lee started as a junior clerk with the company but is now **on the up and up**: he may even become the manager.*

**114.14  up-and-coming**
starting to become successful (used about people)
*She is an **up-and-coming** actress: I'm sure she will star in many films.*

**114.15  be the making of** someone
help someone to improve and be successful
*Changing his school **was the making of** him: he has become much more confident now.*

**114.16  bring the house down**
be very successful (used about plays and performances)
*The violinist **brought the house down** with his performance of the Beethoven violin concerto.*

**114.17  hit the jackpot**
be very successful (usually in a competition where money or valuable prizes are offered)
*Henry Small **hit the jackpot** in the new quiz competition on TV and won over £50,000.*

**114.18  strike oil**
achieve great (and sudden) success (often unexpected success in business)
*He started his business only a few years ago and **struck oil** last week when he sold it for a great deal of money.*

**114.19  make a killing**
suddenly have a lot of success (usually in a business deal, etc.)
*Mr Hilton **made a killing** on the stock market: he bought a lot of shares when the price was low and sold them when the price went very high.*

**114.20  hit the mark**
be successful (as a result of good judgement or planning)
*The small company **hit the mark** with its new product because it was just what the public wanted.*

**114.21  do the trick**
achieve the result one wants, have the desired effect
*"This medicine should **do the trick** and soon cure you," Dr Wright said.*

**114.22  work/do wonders for** someone/something
be extremely successful in its effects on someone/something
*The effective methods the new manager is employing are **working wonders for** the company: we've already doubled our production.*

**114.23 home and dry**
successful, having reached a point beyond the possibility of failure
*He is **home and dry** with his new invention. A large manufacturer has decided to produce it.*

**114.24 weather the storm**
successfully survive a difficult period
*Their marriage went through a difficult period, and they were separated for some time, but now they seem to have **weathered the storm** and are together again.*

**114.25 all to the good**
to someone's benefit
*The time when I didn't have a job was **all to the good**, in fact. It gave me the chance to write a successful novel.*

**114.26 win/carry the day**
be successful (especially in winning over opinions or winning a vote)
*I'm sure the people against capital punishment will **win the day** if they present their case well.*

**114.27 beat someone hollow**
easily defeat someone
*He **beat** all his opponents **hollow** and easily won every match he played.*

**114.28 get the better of someone/something**
beat someone/something, overcome someone/something in a struggle
*The boxer gradually **got the better of** his opponent and at the end of the fight he was clearly the winner.*

**114.29 come out on top**
win, be the successful one (among a number of participants)
*Although there were a lot of applicants, Henry Low was the one who **came out on top** and got the job.*

**114.30 wipe the floor with someone**
beat someone easily or thoroughly
*His performance in the tennis final was excellent — he really **wiped the floor with** his opponent.*

**114.31 hold one's own**
do as well as others
*It's too early yet to say if Henry will go into the next round of the chess championship. However, at the moment he seems to be **holding his own**.*

**114.32 keep one's end up**
do one's share for the success of a group, team, etc.
*Although Linda wasn't the best player in the team, she played an important part in their victory and certainly **kept her end up**.*

**114.33 beat someone at his/her own game**
do better than a person in his own special field of activity
*When you are dealing with that man, you should use his methods and try to **beat him at his own game**.*

**114.34 romp home**
easily win a race, game, election, etc.
*He **romped home** by a big majority in the elections.*

**114.35 have a good run for one's money**
be as successful as one can reasonably expect to be, be rather lucky

*Our business has **had a good run for its money**. However, future prospects are bad, and it may be time now to sell the business.*

114.36 **Every dog has his day**
Anybody can be successful at some time or other
*Every dog has his day but sooner or later he's bound to run into trouble.*

114.37 **have** one's **moments**
have (short) periods of success
*Even though he was not playing at his best, the champion still **had his moments** during the match.*

114.38 **track record**
previous successes and failures, known quality of performance
*The new president's **track record** is very impressive: he has been successful in all the different posts he has held.*

114.39 **make-or-break**
very important, and likely to result in either complete success or complete failure
*In a **make-or-break** effort, the Prime Minister has decided to take on the responsibility for solving the problem.*

114.40 **at stake**
that can be won or lost
*There is a lot **at stake** in this contract. If we win it, we'll make a fortune. If we lose it, we may go out of business.*

## 115. PRESENCE

115.1 **put in an appearance**
attend (perhaps briefly) a meeting, a party, etc. because it is one's duty to attend
*I'd better **put in an appearance** at the meeting because all my friends expect me to attend.*

115.2 **in the flesh**
in real life (i.e. not on the screen or in a picture)
*I saw the Queen **in the flesh** the other day. She looked even better than in her photographs.*

115.3 **(as) large as life**
actually there, present in person (usually used to show surprise at seeing someone)
*There was William, **as large as life!** I was very surprised to see him.*

115.4 **on the spot**
present at the actual time and place where something happens
*I was **on the spot** when the accident happened and saw everything that took place.*

115.5 **in the public eye**
Opposite: **out of the public eye**
well-known in public, often appearing in public
*The new government minister is always **in the public eye**. Almost every day you see him on television or read about him in the newspapers.*

115.6    **wait in the wings**
be present and ready to do something, especially to take over someone
else's job, etc.
*Don't think you can get away with careless work. There are a number of people
waiting in the wings for your job.*

# 116. ABSENCE

116.1    **behind the scenes**
out of sight, out of public view
*John does a lot of work behind the scenes. People do not realise how much of the
club's success is due to him.*

116.2    **as soon as/when/whenever** someone's **back is turned**
when someone is not looking or not present to know what is happening
*As soon as the boss's back is turned, the typists stop working and talk to each other
instead.*

116.3    **a grass widow**
a woman whose husband is temporarily absent
*Jane's husband is away on a business trip, and so she'll be a grass widow for three
weeks.*

# 117. APPEAR, COME

117.1    **turn up like a bad penny**
appear unexpectedly or after a long absence (can be used to refer to
someone or something unwelcome, but often used humorously)
*Harry was at the party, though he wasn't invited. He keeps turning up like a bad
penny.*

117.2    **Look what the cat's brought in** $\boxed{!}$
See who's just appeared! (used humorously)
*Good heavens! Look what the cat's brought in! It's John Hall!*

117.3    **It's about time**
used when someone/something that is late eventually appears
*Here's the bus coming at last. It's about time, too, we've been waiting almost an
hour.*

117.4    **Talk/speak of the devil!**
used when a person being talked about suddenly appears (rather
impolite or humorous)
*Speak of the devil! That's Harry who's just come in. Hello, Harry, we were just
talking about you.*

# 118. DISAPPEAR, LEAVE

118.1    **go off/disappear into the blue**
disappear, leave without any warning
*Paul just went off into the blue without saying a word to anyone.*

118.2    **give** someone **the slip**
avoid or escape from someone
*The thief managed to give the police the slip by leaving through a door at the back
of the building.*

118.3 **do a bunk** [!]
disappear without telling anyone
*Mr Lee said he would stay in the hotel until the next day, but then he **did a bunk** and left without paying.*

118.4 **take to** one's **heels**
run away
*As soon as the gang of youths approached, David **took to his heels**.*

118.5 **show a clean pair of heels**
escape from someone by running
*A group of men ran after him, but he **showed them a clean pair of heels** and escaped.*

118.6 **make a bolt for it**
try to escape by running
*When the thieves were discovered, they **made a bolt for it**, but were soon caught.*

118.7 **make a break for it**
try to escape (from prison, etc.)
*Several prisoners tried to **make a break for it** in the thick fog.*

118.8 **make tracks**
depart, leave
*We ought to be **making tracks** now: it's getting quite late.*

118.9 **make** oneself **scarce**
keep out of the way
*Susan **made herself scarce** when the guests arrived at her parents' party. She felt far too shy to speak to them.*

## 119. ADDITION

119.1 **into the bargain**
in addition, besides
*Poor John hurt his leg in the playground. Then the next day he twisted his ankle **into the bargain**.*

119.2 **for good measure**
in addition, to make sure
*He told me to be quiet and then **for good measure** held his finger to my lips.*

119.3 **over and above** something
in addition to something
*Mr Lee takes charge of the school football team **over and above** his normal teaching duties.*

119.4 **on top of** something
in addition to something (which should already be sufficient)
*Is it customary to tip waiters **on top of** the service charge?*

## 120. SELF, FAMILY

120.1 **number one**
oneself
*He doesn't care about other people. He just wants to look after **number one**; himself.*

120.2   **you and yours**
        you and your family
        *Best wishes to **you and yours**. I hope they are all well.*

120.3   one's **own flesh and blood**
        one's relations, a member of one's family
        *She's **our own flesh and blood**, and so we have a duty to help her when she's in trouble.*

120.4   one's **better half**
        one's husband or wife (used humorously)
        *My **better half** said we ought to go out to the cinema, so here we are!*

## 121. DEFINING, IDENTIFYING

121.1   **(not) put** one's **finger** on something
        (not) identify, name, discover something exactly (usually used in the negative)
        *I can't just **put my finger on** what is wrong with the engine.*

121.2   **in so many words**
        according to the actual meaning of what was said, not the actual words used
        *He said **in so many words** that he had been a complete failure in the job — but, of course, those weren't his exact words.*

121.3   **stick/stand out a mile**
        be very obvious, be easily noticed
        *You can easily find Tommy in this photograph. He's so tall; he **stands out a mile**.*

121.4   **put** one's **(own) stamp** on something
        change something according to one's own characteristics or preferences
        *Christine has really **put her own stamp** on that committee. They do things in the way she likes them to be done.*

## 122. ORDER

122.1   **fall into place**
        become clear, become properly understood (according to its place in a complete situation)
        *As soon as the detective discovered certain facts, everything **fell into place**, and he realised who had committed the crime.*

122.2   **take turns at** doing something/**take it in turns to** do something
        do something in order, go one after the other
        *On our camping holiday, all the family **took turns at** cooking.*

122.3   **in turn**
        in order, one after the other
        *The instructions are simple: if we follow each step **in turn** we shall soon finish the job.*

122.4   **(all) shipshape and Bristol fashion**
        neat and tidy
        *The large room where the boys slept was **all shipshape and Bristol fashion** for the visitors' inspection. It was tidier than I had ever seen it before.*

## 123. DISORDER

123.1 **put the cart before the horse**
do something in the wrong order
*Why don't you discuss the causes of crime rather than punishment? You're putting the cart before the horse.*

123.2 **all over the shop**
disordered, everywhere
*Everything in the room was all over the shop when I returned. In fact, the whole house was in a mess.*

123.3 **upside-down**
in disorder
*Paula turned everything in the house upside-down when she was trying to find her missing necklace.*

123.4 **do/make/go the rounds**
visit a number of people or places in turn
*The doctor does the rounds of his patients every day, visiting them all in turn.*

## 124. LOCATION

124.1 **keep** someone **at arm's length**
keep someone at a distance, avoid too much contact with someone
*Mary kept James at arm's length because she felt he wanted to be too friendly.*

124.2 **the back of beyond**
a remote place, far away from a town, etc.
*It's difficult to get to their house. There's no public transport — they live in the back of beyond.*

124.3 **off the beaten track**
far away from other people, in a lonely place
*His farm is off the beaten track. It is at least two miles from the main road.*

124.4 **search/hunt/etc. high and low**
search/hunt/etc. everywhere
*I've searched high and low for my keys and can't find them anywhere.*

124.5 **from pillar to post**
from one place to another
*When the war came, they had to leave their home. They wandered from place to place, driven from pillar to post.*

124.6 **cheek by jowl**
side by side, very close together
*The people in the huts on the hillside are living cheek by jowl, and often there are quarrels and fights.*

124.7 **on** someone's **doorstep**
very near (the place where someone lives, etc.)
*Does Ron really live in Elm Row? That's just on my doorstep. It can't be more than a mile down the road.*

124.8 **a stone's throw (away)**
very near (used only for talking about short distances)
*Mary and her friend live in the same street, only a stone's throw from each other.*

124.9 **within an inch of**
very near, very close to (failure, disaster, success, etc.)
*John came **within an inch of** disaster when his car skidded off the road.*

124.10 **a hair's breadth**
a very short distance (used also to show amounts, actions, etc.)
*The lightning missed the house **by a hair's breadth**, and everyone had a narrow escape.*

124.11 **within striking distance**
fairly near
*The commander said. "We can't attack yet — the enemy are still too far away. But tomorrow we should be **within striking distance**."*

124.12 **bring up the rear**
follow at the back, be last
*I led the procession and Charles **brought up the rear**.*

## 125. DIRECTION

125.1 **follow** one's **nose**
go straight on (usually used when directing someone to a certain place)
*Don't turn left or right. Just **follow your nose** and go straight on. You'll find the post office.*

125.2 **as the crow flies**
in a straight line, direct (usually used when measuring distance)
*It's 20 miles to London **as the crow flies** but about 25 miles by road.*

125.3 **make a bee-line for** something
go straight toward something
*Tom **made a bee-line for** the food as soon as he arrived at the party.*

## 126. SPEED

126.1 **go/run/do** something **flat out**
go/run/do something as fast as one can
*This car will **do** 160 kilometres per hour if I drive it **flat out**.*

126.2 **go/drive/etc. hell for leather** ⚠️
move very fast
*You'll have to **drive hell for leather** to get this message to the soldiers in time. The enemy are approaching very fast.*

126.3 **run for** one's **life**
run as quickly as one can (to save oneself)
***Run for your life!** The roof's falling in!*

126.4 **spread like wildfire**
spread from one person to another extremely fast (usually used about news, gossip, etc.)
*The news of the victory **spread** through the country **like wildfire**.*

126.5 **make short work of** something/someone
deal very quickly with something/someone
*They were so hungry after a day's walking that they **made** very **short work of** their supper.*

**126.6** **go like a bomb**
run very well, go very fast (generally used about cars, etc.)
*Mr Lee's car is going like a bomb since he had it serviced at the garage.*

**126.7** **get/go through** something **like a dose of salts**
finish something very quickly
*With your experience, you'll do this job very quickly. You'll get through it like a dose of salts.*

**126.8** **like the clappers** ⚠
very fast
*Mr Robson drove like the clappers to get to London in time for his appointment.*

**126.9** **at the double**
very quickly, as fast as one can (often used in commands)
*Now then, at the double! We have no time to waste.*

**126.10** **at a rate of knots**
very fast
*I whistled for my dog and he came from the far end of the field at a rate of knots.*

**126.11** **by/in leaps and bounds**
very quickly (often used to show successful or rapid progress)
*James is progressing by leaps and bounds and has now almost mastered this work.*

**126.12** **at quite a lick** ⚠
very fast
*That motor-boat in the harbour must be travelling at quite a lick. It has passed several much larger craft.*

**126.13** **(at) full pelt**
very fast, as quickly as possible
*The children ran full pelt as soon as they saw the teacher approaching.*

**126.14** **thick and fast**
a lot and often
*Orders for the new computer poured in thick and fast following the advertising campaign.*

**126.15** **step on it**
go faster
*Step on it, we've only two minutes left to catch the train.*

**126.16** **before you could say Jack Robinson/in the twinkling of an eye**
very quickly, immediately
*Someone telephoned Caroline, and before you could say Jack Robinson/in the twinkling of an eye, she was dressed and ready to go out.*

**126.17** **on the spur of the moment**
suddenly, without previous thought or planning
*I didn't have time to think about Henry's proposal, but I agreed to it on the spur of the moment.*

**126.18** **at a stroke**
all at once, in a single action
*Six workers were sent home at a stroke. No one expected such harsh action to be taken.*

**126.19** **right/straight away**
immediately
*Don't worry! I'll deal with the matter right away. You won't have to wait longer than five minutes.*

126.20 **in two/a couple of shakes**
very soon, very quickly
*Tell them I'm coming straight away. I'll be there **in a couple of shakes**.*

126.21 **shake a leg** !
hurry up
***Shake a leg** there! You'll miss your breakfast if you don't get up!*

126.22 **get a move on**
hurry up
***Get a move on!** We're already late for the meeting.*

126.23 **get** one's **skates on**
hurry up
*If we **get our skates on**, we can be at the cinema in time.*

126.24 **Make it snappy!**
Be quick!
*Two beers, please. **Make it snappy**. We're in a hurry.*

126.25 **against the clock/against time**
trying hard to finish within a given time limit
*The builders are working **against the clock** to finish the house in time.*


# 127. STARTING

127.1 **all set**
ready to begin (to do) something
*"Are you **all set** to leave now?" "Yes, we've packed all our belongings."*

127.2 **get cracking**
start doing something without wasting any time, get busy
*I'll **get cracking** with this work this afternoon, so I should finish it by evening.*

127.3 **quick off the mark**
quick to begin something (without wasting time)
*If we are **quick off the mark**, we can be in Newton by ten o'clock.*

127.4 **start/keep the ball rolling**
start something, keep something going (e.g. a discussion, a game in which everyone takes a turn)
*Let's tell jokes. Who would like to **start the ball rolling** and tell the first joke?*

127.5 **get** something **off the ground**
get something started, start to put an idea into practice (usually used about a plan or design)
*This is a very interesting invention, but it will take a lot of money to **get it off the ground**.*

127.6 **start from scratch**
start from the beginning, start from nothing
*All our business records were destroyed in the fire, and so we had to **start from scratch** and build them up again.*

127.7 **(right) from the word go**
from the very beginning
*We've had problems with this computer **right from the word go**.*

127.8 **all along**
all the time, from the very beginning
*I knew **all along** that Freda would never marry Willie. They never seemed right for each other.*

127.9 **set the wheels in motion**
start a process, arrange for a process to start
*Mr White has **set the wheels in motion** for the new production of "Oliver Twist". He has already started to hold auditions.*

127.10 **break the ice**
do something to overcome the shyness or formality in a situation, begin to talk, etc. at a party or meeting
*Helen was the first person to **break the ice** by telling us what happened to her on the way to the party.*

127.11 **(be off to) a flying start**
(make) a very good beginning
*Janet's **got off to a flying start** in her new job and everyone is very pleased with her.*

127.12 **start off on the right/wrong foot**
start well/badly
*William **started off on the wrong foot** by having an argument with the manager on his first day at work.*

127.13 **back to the drawing-board**
necessary to/being obliged to start all over again (especially a project or design)
*The new engine doesn't perform very well, so it's **back to the drawing-board**. We'll have to start all over again.*

127.14 **be back to square one**
have to start something all over again
*John was building a small house, but it was blown down in the storm. Consequently, he was **back to square one** and had to start all over again.*

127.15 **The wheel has come/turned full circle.**
The situation has returned to what it was before.
*The wheel has turned full circle and some farmers are using horses again instead of tractors.*

127.16 **go off at half-cock**
start too early, begin before everything is ready (and thus fail)
*Our advertising campaign isn't really ready yet. If we begin it now, it will probably **go off at half-cock**.*

127.17 **jump the gun**
start too soon, begin something before one ought to begin it
*When Mr and Mrs Smith moved into their new house, they really **jumped the gun**. They moved in a month before the date mentioned in the written agreement.*

## 128. FINISHING, STOPPING

128.1 **grind to a halt**
stop noisily (used of vehicles)
*The driver applied the emergency brakes and the train **ground to a halt**.*

**128.2  call it a day/night**

decide it is time to stop doing something that day/night

*We'd better **call it a day**. We're all very tired and must get to bed.*

**128.3  pack it in** $\boxed{!}$

stop doing something

*Can't you stop playing that trumpet? I can't think because of the noise. **Pack it in**, please!*

**128.4  shut up shop**

stop working

*It's time I **shut up shop** and went out to meet my friends.*

**128.5  down tools**

stop working without giving much warning, suddenly go on strike

*The men **downed tools** this morning without notice. They said their wages were not good enough.*

**128.6  nip something in the bud**

stop something before it has really started

*When the government heard that there was trouble in one province, they sent the army to **nip it in the bud** before it could spread to other parts.*

**128.7  give someone the boot/push** $\boxed{!}$

dismiss someone from a job

*James admitted he had cheated the company out of £500, so he was **given the boot**.*

**128.8  get the axe**

be stopped, be closed down

*There was great anger in the area as several factories **got the axe** and thousands of workers became unemployed.*

**128.9  go by the board**

be stopped, be abandoned (often used about someone's plans)

*Our holiday plans **went by the board** when we had to spend all our money on repairs to the house.*

**128.10  cut something/someone short**

stop something before it is finished, stop someone talking before he/she has finished.

*Winifred **cut** her husband **short** by telling him not to talk in such a stupid way.*

**128.11  over and done with**

completely finished

*That part of my life is **over and done with**: I never want to return to the places where I lived then.*

**128.12  all over bar the shouting**

almost finished, with the result certain

*When the score was 3–0 with only five minutes left, the match was **all over bar the shouting**.*

**128.13  the kiss of death**

something apparently positive that, in fact, spoils what it is intended to help

*The government's approval was **the kiss of death** to the politician. People no longer believed that he was independent, as he claimed.*

**128.14  run/take its course**

continue until its natural end, without interference, delay, etc. (used especially about illnesses)

*There's nothing much we can do about the common cold. It just has to **take its course.***

128.15 **break the back of** something

do the greatest or most difficult part of something

*We've **broken the back of** this job and should soon complete it.*

128.16 someone's **swan song**

an author's/artist's/actor's musician's last work before dying or retiring

*That performance was the actor's **swan song**. He is to retire next week.*

# 129. TIME

129.1 **for good (and all)**

for ever, permanently, completely

*I stopped smoking **for good and all** about three months ago, and I feel much better for it.*

129.2 **donkey's years**

a long time

*Tom and Paula hadn't seen each other for **donkey's years**, and so they had a lot to talk about.*

129.3 **days on end**

continuously for many days

*It snowed for **days on end**. We thought it would never stop!*

129.4 **round-the-clock**

all day and night, for 24 hours a day

*By using a telephone answering machine, the firm provides a **round-the-clock** service. You can order goods at any time of the day or night.*

129.5 **day in, day out**

all the time, continuously, one day after the other

*Mabel did everything Charlie asked her to do, **day in, day out** for twenty years.*

129.6 **make a night/day of it**

spend the whole night/day enjoying oneself

*Mr and Mrs Small were enjoying themselves so much that they decided to **make a night of it** and not come home till morning.*

129.7 **at one fell swoop**

all at the same time

*We lost three of our staff **at one fell swoop** today. They all left and got other jobs.*

129.8 **on the dot**

punctually, on time, exactly at a certain time

*Helen arrived **on the dot** — not a minute early, not a minute late.*

129.9 **to date**

so far, up to now

*Here are the figures for the total sales **to date**.*

129.10 **with it**

modern in behaviour, etc., alert and attentive

*Mrs Lee is over seventy, but she's very much **with it** and loves pop music.*

129.11 **in the long term/run**

at the end of a long period of time

***In the long run**, this project will be profitable for the company but it will lose considerable money for a short while.*

129.12 **at the eleventh hour**
at the last minute, just before it is too late (often used about a rescue)
*Our business was saved **at the eleventh hour** when we got a huge contract from abroad: it came just in time.*

129.13 **in the nick of time**
at the last possible moment (to avoid or prevent something bad)
*The army arrived **in the nick of time** and the town was saved.*

129.14 **first thing**
early in the morning, before doing anything else
*I do my exercises **first thing**, before I have my breakfast.*

129.15 **burn the midnight oil**
work or study late at night
*John takes so much work home from the office that he has to **burn the midnight oil** to complete it.*

129.16 **at all hours**
at unusual or irregular times, especially late at night and early in the morning
*Mr Kassim keeps his shop open **at all hours**.*

129.17 **in the offing**
about to happen
*Mr Shaw knew that promotion was **in the offing** when he was praised for all the hard work he had done.*

129.18 **hang fire**
wait, be postponed, be delayed
*Mr Simpson decided to let the purchase of the house **hang fire** in the hope that the price would come down.*

129.19 **play for time**
delay doing something (and keep discussions going) in the hope that the situation will improve
*They've sent us a large bill, but we can't pay it now — we'll have to **play for time**. Tell them we'll send the money soon.*

129.20 **cut it fine/close**
leave hardly enough time to do something
*We're **cutting it** very **fine** and will have to hurry if we are to catch the plane.*

129.21 **steal a march on** someone
gain an advantage over someone (usually unfairly by doing something early or without warning)
*Mr Green **stole a march on** his competitors by suddenly reducing his prices.*

129.22 **A lot of water has flowed/gone under the bridge**
It's no use thinking of things now in the same way as one thought of them in the past; it's time to forget the past
*You shouldn't be angry about something that happened twenty years ago. **A lot of water has flowed under the bridge** since then.*

129.23 **a flash in the pan**
a very brief success which is unlikely to last or be repeated
*Ann's success in the play is only **a flash in the pan**, I'm sure it won't be repeated.*

129.24 **a nine days' wonder**
something which causes much interest for a short time only before

being forgotten

*The huge export order was **a nine days' wonder** and was quickly forgotten, even though it resulted in considerable public interest at the time.*

## 130. FREQUENCY

130.1 **nine times out of ten**

almost always

*Jane is almost always right — **nine times out of ten**, I would say.*

130.2 **as often as not**

usually, quite often

***As often as not**, the side which scores first wins the match.*

130.3 **more than** someone **has had hot dinners** [!]

a lot of times

*I've visited more foreign countries **than** you've **had hot dinners**.*

130.4 **few and far between**

rare, infrequent

*Sunsets as beautiful as this are **few and far between**. It's many years since I saw one like it.*

130.5 **once in a blue moon**

seldom, hardly ever

*It's remarkable for someone so young to win the competition — it's the kind of thing that happens **once in a blue moon**.*

## 131. PAST TIME

131.1 **put/turn the clock back**

return to the conditions of a previous time, act in an old-fashioned way

*It's no good wishing that everyone travelled on horseback. You can't **put the clock back**.*

131.2 **of old** (often **days of old**)

in the past, belonging to or living in previous times

*In days **of old**, the only way of getting about the country was on horseback.*

131.3 **become a thing of the past**

be something no longer used, observed or practised

*The government is determined to make racial intolerance **a thing of the past**.*

131.4 **know** someone **of old**

have had experience of dealing with someone for a long time (often used in a derogatory way)

*I **know** David Smith **of old**. He has never been a man to be trusted.*

131.5 **out of date**

no longer used, belonging to a previous time

*The dictionary you are using is **out of date**: many words have been added to the language since it was published.*

131.6 **old hat**

old-fashioned (used in a derogatory way)

*Those ideas are **old hat** now: no one agrees with them any longer.*

131.7 **behind the times**

old-fashioned

*People will think we are **behind the times** if we don't modernise our shop.*

131.8   **a stick-in-the-mud**
        someone who is old-fashioned and refuses to change (used in a
        derogatory way)
        *Mr Jones is **an** old **stick-in-the-mud**: you'll never persuade him to change at all.*

131.9   **the good old days**
        a former time which seems better than the present (but probably was
        not so)
        *"I remember when there were no cars," the old man sighed. "Those were **the good
        old days.**"*

## 132.   PRESENT TIME

132.1   **a sign of the times**
        a typical example of what is happening at present
        *It's a **sign of the times** when cars are used for very short journeys. People don't
        want to walk any more.*

132.2   **up-to-the-minute**
        very recent, modern, fashionable
        *Have you got any **up-to-the-minute** information on the developments which are
        taking place?*

132.3   **up-to-date**
        modern, in fashion
        *Their factory is very modern and all the machinery is absolutely **up-to-date**.*

132.4   **all the rage/fashion**
        very fashionable, very popular
        *"These dresses are **all the rage**. They're very popular with both young and old,"
        the salesgirl told us.*

## 133.   DEGREE, EMPHASIS

133.1   **like blazes/mad/anything** [!]
        very quickly, very hard, very much (often used to emphasise actions)
        *I worked **like mad** last night to finish my essay in time.*

133.2   **to the nth degree**
        to the greatest possible degree, completely, entirely
        *The photographs Anne Lawson takes are superb **to the nth degree**.*

133.3   **from head to foot/toe**
        completely (used of clothes, skin, etc.)
        *After I went swimming, I had mosquito bites **from head to toe**.*

133.4   **up to the neck/ears in** something
        completely
        *Poor Timothy Brown's **up to his neck in** debt: he owes money to everyone!*

133.5   **hook, line and sinker**
        completely (usually used after verbs like "catch" and "fall for")
        *Ann fell for your story about the pink elephant **hook, line and sinker**. She believed
        every word of it.*

133.6   **go the whole hog**
        do something completely (when one has already done it in part)
        *It's now three o'clock in the morning: we may as well **go the whole hog** and stay
        out until dawn.*

133.7 **through and through**
completely, in every way
*Henry is a gentleman **through and through**: he's always courteous and polite.*

133.8 **from top to bottom**
completely
*He was covered **from top to bottom** in red paint.*

133.9 **well and truly**
completely (usually used before a past participle)
*The car is **well and truly** smashed: it's totally beyond repair.*

133.10 **ever so**
very
*Mabel looks **ever so** well after her long holiday.*

133.11 **not half**
very much
*"Do you like this cake?" "**Not half!** It's just like my mother used to make!"*

133.12 **far and away**
very much, by a long way, easily
*This novel is **far and away** the best book I've read this year.*

133.13 **every inch a man/woman/etc.**
a man, etc. in every way (usually used to show a good quality)
*Roger is **every inch a gentleman**: he's always thoughtful and courteous.*

133.14 **and how!**
that's certainly true; very much so (usually used to show strong agreement)
*"Mr Law's car goes very fast." "**And how!**"*

133.15 **go over the top**
act in an extreme way, go too far, behave too wildly
*William got so excited when making his speech that he **went** completely **over the top**. He made some wild statements which were simply untrue.*

133.16 **with a vengeance**
very much, very thoroughly, more than necessary
*Our company once had no serious competitors. But now all the other companies are competing **with a vengeance**.*

133.17 **at the (very) outside**
at the most
*This beer is very strong, and I advise you not to drink more than two glasses **at the very outside**.*

133.18 **the biggest/worst/etc. person/thing/etc. under the sun**
the biggest/worst/etc. of all
*He's **the biggest** liar **under the sun**: you can't believe a word he says.*

133.19 **out-and-out**
complete, thorough (often used in a derogatory way)
*Charlie's an **out-and-out** rascal.*

133.20 **only the half of it**
only a part of something, not the whole of something
*There's a lot more to the argument than that. You know **only the half of it**.*

133.21 **to cap/crown everything/it all**
(used to show surprise) finally, on top of everything

*Peter was boasting about his strength all evening and, **to cap it all**, he claimed he could even lift a car.*

133.22 **laugh/cry/talk/shout/etc.** one's **head off**
laugh/cry/talk/shout etc. very much indeed
*We all **laughed our heads off** at the comedian's jokes.*

133.23 **armed to the teeth**
fully armed
*The sergeant was **armed to the teeth** and prepared to fight against everyone.*

133.24 **make all the difference**
cause an improvement (so that someone/something succeeds instead of failing)
*A short rest before the big race **made all the difference** to Ali's performance, and he won easily.*

133.25 **to the letter**
exactly, to the most complete degree
*John obeyed his father's instructions **to the letter**.*

133.26 **be/come within an ace of** doing something
almost do something, very nearly succeed in doing something
*I **came within an ace of** winning the tennis tournament but was beaten in the very last game.*

133.27 **by the skin of** one's **teeth/by a whisker**
only just, very narrowly
*Robert won **by the skin of his teeth/by a whisker**. He was very nearly beaten.*

## 134. QUANTITY, AMOUNT

134.1 **The sky's the limit.**
There is (almost) no limit to the possibilities.
*He has so much money that he can buy anything he wants. **The sky's the limit**.*

134.2 **across the board**
applying everywhere or to everyone
*A ten per cent increase in pay was offered **across the board**.*

134.3 **one and all**
everyone (used in public speeches)
*Good evening, **one and all**. I hope you'll enjoy the concert tonight.*

134.4 **to a man/to the last man**
everyone included
*The soldiers all volunteered for the operation **to a man**.*

134.5 **all in**
everything included
*The meal cost £10 **all in**, including wine and coffee.*

134.6 **bag and baggage**
with everything, with all one's belongings
*They've moved to a cottage by the sea for the summer, **bag and baggage**.*

134.7 **thin on the ground**
Opposite: **thick on the ground**
scarce, insufficient
*Trade is bad and customers are **thin on the ground**.*

134.8 **a hundred and one**
a lot, many
*There are **a hundred and one** reasons why you should agree to what he proposes.*

134.9 **no end of**
a lot of
*Bert had **no end of** excuses for being late.*

134.10 **ever so much**
very much
*Thank you **ever so much** for such a lovely present. It's just what I wanted.*

134.11 **hand over fist**
in large amounts (usually used about money)
*He has a very good business and is making money **hand over fist**.*

134.12 **full/short measure**
the full amount/less than the full amount
*Betty was given **short measure** at the local shop the other day and won't go there any more.*

134.13 **the lion's share**
the most, the biggest part
*He left a lot of money when he died and his eldest son got **the lion's share**.*

134.14 **cover much/a lot of ground**
deal with a lot of subjects, etc. (usually used to refer to books, lectures, etc.)
*We have **covered a lot of ground** in our discussion this evening.*

134.15 **in dribs and drabs**
in small amounts at irregular times
*Would you prefer to wait to receive the whole report or shall I send it to you **in dribs and drabs?***

134.16 **a drop in the ocean/bucket**
a tiny part (of what is needed, etc.)
*The money we've given to the charity is only **a drop in the ocean**, but even small amounts help.*

134.17 **next to nothing**
almost nothing, scarcely anything at all
*Paul arrived in London with **next to nothing**: now he owns several restaurants.*

## 135. COMPARING: SIMILARITIES

135.1 **(very) much of a muchness**
all similar, not very different in any way (usually used in a derogatory way to refer to the poor quality of things or people)
*The candidates at this year's examinations were **much of a muchness**. None of them was outstanding in any way.*

135.2 **It's six of one and half a dozen of the other.**
It doesn't make any difference (because the two alternatives are almost the same).
*Whether we eat at this restaurant or that doesn't really matter. **It's six of one and half a dozen of the other**.*

135.3 **a chip off the old block**
someone who is like one of his/her parents (especially in behaviour)
*Jonathan Strange is **a** real **chip off the old block**. He argues about things in just the way his father did.*

135.4 **be the spitting image of** someone
look very much like someone
*Mary and her twin sister **are the spitting image of** each other.*

135.5 **neck and neck**
equal, level (in a race)
*Peter and John were **neck and neck** all the way in the race and were even level at the finishing line.*

135.6 **There's nothing in it.**
Both are level or equal.
***There's nothing in it** between these two computers. Both are extremely good.*

135.7 **level pegging**
equal in progress or movement (usually used about competitions)
*Our sales so far this year are **level pegging** with those at the same time last year.*

135.8 **go hand in hand** with something
be closely connected, have a direct relationship (with something)
*Crime and poverty often **go hand in hand**: get rid of poverty and there'll be fewer crimes.*

135.9 **as broad as it is long**
the same (however one thinks about it)
*I don't care whether you pay part of the bill now or pay the complete bill later: it's **as broad as it's long**.*

135.10 **take a leaf out of** someone's **book**
act like someone else, follow someone's example
*Mary ought to **take a leaf out of** Sandra's **book** and apply for money to go on a training course.*

135.11 **run true to form**
behave in the same way as one normally behaves
*Edward seems to be **running true to form** and talking at great length.*

## 136. COMPARING: DIFFERENCES

136.1 **a far cry from** something
very different from something (in the past)
*We flew to Hong Kong in seventeen hours. It's **a far cry from** going there by sea, as people used to do a long time ago.*

136.2 **as different as chalk and cheese**
very different
*Peter and his brother are **as different as chalk and cheese**. You wouldn't believe they belonged to the same family.*

136.3 **be worlds/poles apart**
be very different (especially in attitudes, opinions, etc.)
*Old Mr Small and young Mr Fields are **worlds/poles apart** in their attitudes: one belongs to the older generation and the other to the new.*

136.4 **the odd man out**
someone (or something) that is different from the others in a group
*Ted was **the odd man out** and was the only one who voted for the resolution.*

136.5 **not be a patch on** someone/something
not be nearly as good as someone/something
*Your car **isn't a patch on** Mrs Lee's. It won't go half as fast and it's much smaller.*

136.6 **be streets ahead of** something
be much better than something
*Our new products are **streets ahead of** anything else on the market at present.*

136.7 **have nothing on** someone/something
not be as good as someone else/something else
*I'm afraid my car **has nothing on** yours for speed. Yours is much faster.*

136.8 **be/stand head and shoulders above** someone/something
be much better than someone/something
*He is a born leader and **stands head and shoulders above** everyone else in the government.*

136.9 **run rings round** someone
be very much better than someone (especially in a contest)
*Philip is a much better player than James and can **run rings round** him.*

136.10 **The grass is greener on the other side (of the fence).**
Things always seem to be better in another place or for someone else (but often are not really better).
*Alec thinks he would be better off if he moved to another company. But **the grass always looks greener on the other side of the fence:** I don't think he would really be better off.*

136.11 **separate the sheep from the goats**
distinguish between the good and the bad, etc.
*The first thing to do with all these applicants is to **separate the sheep from the goats** and call only the good ones for an interview.*

136.12 **the other side of the coin**
the opposite point of view, factors in a situation different or opposite to those already mentioned
*The government has managed to reduce prices. **The other side of the coin,** however, is that there is now a lot of unemployment.*

## 137. REASON

137.1 **by virtue of** something
because of something, as a result of something
*Mrs Hickson has been promoted in her job **by virtue of** the good results she achieved.*

137.2 **thanks to** something/someone
as a result of something/someone
***Thanks to** the efforts of the union, the employees are to have a pay rise.*

137.3 **what with . . . and . . .**
because of . . . and . . . (usually used to explain the reasons for something unfortunate happening or not happening)
***What with** the snow **and** the cold winds, crops are likely to be late this year.*

137.4 **the whys and (the) wherefores** (of something)
the reasons (for something)
*The new clerk takes too long over his work because he goes into **the whys and wherefores** of everything.*

137.5    **by the same token**
for the same reason, in the same way
*Mary wouldn't go on the holiday because it was too expensive and, **by the same** **token**, Tim didn't want to go either.*

# 138. CAUSE AND EFFECT

138.1    **what makes** someone **tick**
what causes someone to act or think as he does
*I wish I knew **what makes** Frank **tick**. He does his job as if it were the most important thing in the world for him.*

138.2    **That's the way the cookie crumbles**
That's how things are; there's nothing to be done about it. (often used in a humorous way)
*I'm sorry you'll have to work on Saturday mornings this month, but **that's the** **way the cookie crumbles**. There's no other way of organising things.*

138.3    **kill two birds with one stone**
gain two things with one action, achieve two aims with the same action
*I hope to **kill two birds with one stone** when I go to London. I'll visit our headquarters there and also see an exhibition of paintings.*

138.4    **be banging/beating** one's **head against a brick wall**
have no success with one's efforts, be unable to alter a situation (in spite of trying very hard)
*You'll **be banging your head against a brick wall** if you try to argue with Bill — he just won't listen to you.*

138.5    **(like) water off a duck's back**
something (especially criticism or blame) which has no effect on someone
*Henry's criticism of Mabel was **like water off a duck's back**. She took no notice at all and behaved as she always had done.*

138.6    **cut both ways**
have the same effect on one person as on someone else, have advantages as well as disadvantages, affect two people or two sides (not just the obvious one)
*The manager's criticism of the department **cut both ways**: he dealt with things that were just as much his fault as ours.*

138.7    **come home to roost**
have unpleasant effects resulting from one's own bad actions
*Pauline's carelessness **came home to roost** when her house was badly damaged by fire because of a cigarette she had dropped.*

138.8    **be hoist with** one's **own petard**
be caught oneself in a trap which one has set for someone else
*Mr Simpson persuaded the police to introduce a speed limit on the road past his house. However, he **was hoist with his own petard** when he himself was caught speeding there.*

138.9    **not get** one **anywhere/get** one **nowhere**
not bring about any useful result
*Being too strict as a parent doesn't **get you anywhere**. Your children will only dislike you as they grow older.*

# INDEX OF IDIOMS

Numbers refer to sections not pages

129

**crush**
have a crush on someone   30.8

**cruel**
be cruel to be kind   66.17

**cry**
a far cry from something   136.1

**cue**
take one's cue from someone/
something   63.12

**cuff**
(speak) off the cuff   14.6

**cup**
not/be someone's cup of tea   32.2

**cut**
(take) a short cut   8.4
a cut above the rest   43.6
be cut out for   48.4
Cut it out!   65.9
cut and thrust   98.14
cut something/someone
short   128.10
cut it fine/close   129.20

**daggers**
look daggers at someone   76.21

**Darby**
Darby and Joan   108.8

**dark**
keep/leave someone in the
dark   10.14
keep something dark   97.1

**date**
to date   129.9
out of date   131.5
up-to-date   132.3

**day**
a red-letter day   53.2
win/carry the day   114.26
call it a day/night   128.2
day in, day out   129.5
make a night/day of it   129.6
a nine days' wonder   129.24

**daylights**
beat/knock the (living) daylights out
of someone   68.3

**days**
have seen/known better days   108.4
days on end   129.3
the good old days   131.9

**dead**
wouldn't be seen dead doing
something   32.14
Drop dead!   76.43

**deal**
Big deal!   35.6

**death**
worry someone to death   74.10
tickled pink/to death   79.1
flog something to death   98.20
feel/look like death warmed up!
110.8
catch one's death (of cold)   110.9
will be the death of someone   112.9

**degree**
to the nth degree   133.2

**demand**
in demand   31.1

**dent**
make a dent/hole in something
112.13

**depth**
be/get out of one's depth   2.1

**deserts**
get/receive one's just deserts   66.4

**desired**
leave a lot/much/a great deal/
something to be desired   93.2

**devices**
leave someone to his/her own
devices   60.29

**devil**
a/the devil of a job   7.19
the devil's own job   7.19
give the devil his due   54.2
devil-may-care   74.19
talk/speak of the devil!   117.4

**dick**
a clever dick/Dick   90.12

someone/something   30.10
not believe one's eyes/ears   94.1
Someone's eyes almost/nearly
popped out of his/her head   94.7

**face**
have/make/pull a long face   81.1
laugh at the other side of one's face
81.12
save face   90.8
lose face   91.7
to someone's face   96.15

**fair**
fair and square   58.1
Fair enough!   99.13

**faith**
pin one's hopes/faith on
someone/something   26.4

**fall**
fall all over someone   30.5
go/fall overboard for someone/
something   30.12
fall foul of someone   76.32
fall over oneself   88.2
fall flat   113.9

**Fanny**
(sweet) Fanny Adams   45.8

**far**
far gone   44.11
Far from it!   100.8
far and away   133.12

**fashion**
(all) shipshape and Bristol fashion
122.4
all the rage/fashion   132.4

**fast**
play fast and loose   59.9

**favourite**
a hot favourite   20.6

**fed**
fed up   83.3

**feelings**
have mixed feelings about someone/
something   32.13

**feet**
find one's feet   1.7
have/keep one's feet (set/planted)
(firmly) on the ground   16.2
at someone's feet   60.23
get/have cold feet   74.8
drag one's feet/heels   89.2
throw oneself at the feet of
someone   91.2
fall/land on one's feet   114.7

**fellow**
hail-fellow-well-met   106.18

**fence**
sit on the fence   23.2

**few**
few and far between   130.4

**fiddle**
play second fiddle to someone   51.5

**find**
find something heavy/hard going
7.3

**finger**
get/pull one's finger out   5.23
not lift a finger/hand to help/to do
something   5.30
have/keep one's finger on the pulse
of something   9.11
lay a finger on someone   112.16
(not) put one's finger on something
121.1

**fingers**
all (fingers and) thumbs   2.9
work one's fingers to the bone   5.8
keep/have one's fingers crossed
26.1
get one's fingers burnt   112.14
let something slip through one's
fingers   113.2

**fingertips**
have something at one's fingertips
9.10

**fire**
a ball of fire   6.1
come under fire   39.6

**go-ahead**
  give the O.K/okay/go-ahead  99.6

**goat**
  get someone's goat  76.23

**God**
  honest to God/goodness  58.5
  Good God!  94.17
  For God's sake!  94.18

**gone**
  gone on someone  30.11

**good**
  up to no good  42.2
  They've/We've/etc. never had it so
    good  104.10
  make good  114.4
  all to the good  114.25
  for good (and all)  129.1

**goodness**
  honest to God/goodness  58.5
  for goodness' sake!  94.18

**goose**
  a wild goose chase  47.5
  cook one's (own) goose  112.7

**grace**
  a saving grace  43.13

**granted**
  take something for granted  25.1

**grapes**
  sour grapes  32.15

**grass**
  the grass roots  52.5
  put/send/turn someone out to grass
    108.7
  The grass is greener on the other side
    (of the fence)  136.10

**grave**
  make someone turn over in his/her
    grave  76.35

**Greek**
  It's all Greek to me/him/etc.  10.7

**grief**
  come to grief  113.5

**grin**
  grin and bear it  7.12

**grips**
  get/come to grips with something
    84.11

**groove**
  in a rut/groove  83.2

**ground**
  common ground  64.6
  stand/hold one's ground  84.8
  shift one's ground  98.18
  get something off the ground  127.5
  thin on the ground  134.7
  cover much/a lot of
    ground  134.14

**guess**
  it's anybody's guess  10.8

**gullet**
  stick in someone's throat/gullet
    37.4

**gum**
  up a gum tree  7.23

**gun**
  hold a pistol/gun to someone's head
    65.3
  jump the gun  127.17

**guns**
  going great guns  6.5
  the big guns  50.7
  stick to one's guns  84.9

**guts**
  hate someone's guts  32.5

**guy**
  fall guy  42.7

**hackles**
  make someone's hackles rise  76.6

**hair**
  tear one's hair out  74.7
  get in/into someone's hair  76.24
  Keep your hair/shirt on!  78.5
  let one's hair down  80.2
  not turn a hair  86.2
  make someone's hair stand on
    end  87.9
  a hair of the dog (that bit one)
    101.11

**nothing**

(there is) nothing to it   8.3

There is nothing/little to choose
  between them etc.   23.4

have nothing to do with someone/
  something   34.4

Nothing doing.   36.2

good-for-nothing   45.10

count for nothing   45.11

nothing to write home about   51.2

He'll/I'll/etc. stop at
  nothing   84.3

Nothing of the kind!   100.8

come to nothing   113.6

next to nothing   134.17

there's nothing in it.   135.6

have nothing on someone/
  something   136.7

**number**

someone's number is up   111.5

number one   120.1

**nut**

a hard/tough nut (to crack)   7.20

off one's head/nut/rocker   17.1

do one's nut   76.7

**oats**

sow one's wild oats   80.10

**ocean**

go (and) jump in the river/lake/sea/
  ocean!   76.43

a drop in the ocean/bucket   134.16

**odds**

the odds/chances are   18.5

stack the cards/odds against
  one/someone   63.20

at odds with someone   100.1

over the odds   103.4

**odour**

in bad odour with someone   33.4

**offing**

in the offing   129.17

**often**

as often as not   130.2

**oil**

strike oil   114.18

burn the midnight oil   129.15

**O.K.**

give the O.K./okay/go-ahead   99.6

**old**

of old   131.2

**one**

have it in one   1.11

pull a fast one on someone   59.6

at one   99.2

have one over the eight   101.6

a new one on someone   107.3

be back to square one   127.14

one and all   134.3

**option**

a/the soft option   8.7

**order**

a tall order   7.14

of the first water/magnitude/order
  43.5

**orders**

get one's marching orders   66.8

**out**

out-and-out   133.19

**outside**

at the (very) outside   133.17

**over**

over and above something   119.3

over and done with   128.11

all over bar the shouting   128.12

**overboard**

go/fall overboard for someone/
  something   30.12 & 77.10

**own**

come into one's own   1.9

get one's own back   67.1

hold one's own   114.31

**P's and Q's**

mind/watch one's P's and Q's   74.15

**paces**

put someone/something through
  his/her/its paces   1.13

**pink**
tickled pink/to death   79.1
in the pink   109.3

**pins**
for two pins   65.4

**pipe**
(You can) put that in your pipe and
smoke it!   76.46

**pipeline**
in the pipeline   24.8

**pistol**
hold a pistol/gun to someone's
head   65.3

**pitch**
make a/one's pitch/play for   63.3

**pity**
more's the pity   81.14

**place**
pride of place   50.14
fall into place   122.1

**places**
in high places   50.8

**planks**
as thick as two short planks   4.3

**plate**
give/hand someone/something on a
plate   8.14
have enough/a lot/etc. on one's
plate   61.10

**play**
child's play   8.1
make a/one's pitch/play for   63.3

**please**
if you please   94.21

**pocket**
out of pocket   102.5

**pockets**
line one's (own) pockets   59.16

**point**
not to put too fine a
point on it   58.10
take someone's point   99.7

**poison**
hate someone/something like poison
32.6

**poles**
be worlds/poles apart   136.3

**pot**
take pot luck   21.6
the pot calling the kettle black   39.8

**praises**
sing someone's/something's praises
40.2

**presence**
make one's presence felt   60.14

**pride**
swallow one's pride   91.3

**pros and cons**
(weigh up) the pros and cons   98.15

**proud**
do someone proud   43.11

**punches**
pull one's punches   39.7

**purse-strings**
hold the purse-strings   102.4

**push**
give someone the boot/push   128.7

**put**
would not put it/doing something
past someone   1.15
hard put to it   7.21

**putty**
(like) putty in someone's
hands   63.10

**quantity**
an unknown quantity   10.13

**question**
out of the question   19.1
no question of   20.2
the 64,000 dollar question   50.17
in question   98.16

**quiet**
on the quiet/sly   97.3

**quite**
Quite so!   99.10